AF470060

THE YANKS AT OXFORD

The 1987 Boat Race Controversy

American and British oarsmen continue training at Marlow under Spracklen's guidance without their President McDonald.

THE YANKS AT OXFORD

The 1987 Boat Race Controversy

Alison Gill

The Book Guild Ltd.
Sussex, England

The Book Guild Limited
Temple House
25 High Street
Lewes, Sussex

First published 1991

Set in Baskerville

Typesetting by Dataset
St Leonards-on-Sea, Sussex

Printed in Great Britain by
Antony Rowe Ltd
Chippenham, Wiltshire

British Library Cataloguing in Publication Data

Gill, Alison
The Yanks at Oxford: 1987 boat race controversy
1. London (England). Rowing boats. Racing
I. Title
797. 1409421

ISBN 0 86332 662 5

1

'The mystique of the Boat Race throughout the world is that it represents honesty, fairness and sportsmanship. However, our experiences with the present Oxford University Boat Club hierachy have not shown this to be true. When we saw that the ideals were just a myth the annual event became just another boat race, not the ultimate sporting occasion that it had been built up to be.'
(Jonathan Fish, *The Times*, 7 February 1987).

This impression will remain with five American international oarsmen who were studying at Oxford during 1987. Should their talent have shown them worthy of a place in the 1987 Oxford Boat Race crew, they had hoped to join the thousands of great oarsmen who had in the past helped Oxford to victory in the annual Oxford and Cambridge Boat Race. Instead they found themselves, along with many British oarsmen, fighting against an Establishment in order to uphold the very ideals of 'honesty, fairness and sportsmanship' which they had expected to experience in England.

The controversy was to become the most infamous in the history of the Boat Race, when the five Americans sacrificed the chance not only to earn a Blue but also to row in what was likely to be the fastest Boat Race crew on record. The Americans, in sacrificing such an honour, courageously upheld the banners of justice and fair play which we British have for many years believed ourselves to hold.

The controversy which hit the national and international

news headlines almost daily for four weeks started simply as a selection disagreement over the last two places in the crew. There were three men for two places: Christopher Clark, one of the Americans, Donald McDonald, the President of the boat club, and Tony Ward, both British. Clark had two chances for a place in the crew because he was to be trialled on both sides of the boat. If he rowed bowside Ward was left out; if he rowed strokeside the President would be left out. The crew and the coaches were noticeably adrift in their choice to fill the two places. The crew considered Clark and Ward the superior combination over Clark and McDonald, the coaches' choice, because they believed that Clark had demonstrated his superiority over the President on strokeside on many occasions, and because Clark had also demonstrated his lack of ability on bowside.

Following a set of seat race trials, which they were told were the last trials prior to the crew's selection, Clark's selection on strokeside seemed obvious to the crew because Clark was beaten on bowside by a considerable amount, but beat McDonald on strokeside. The only problem was that this would mean that McDonald, the President, would have to stand down. This was something he had made abundantly clear he was not prepared to do. For the President not to row is unusual but not unheard of. In the history of the Boat Race, those Presidents who have recognised that they shouldn't be in the crew and who have stood down have been applauded by the Press and the public, who appreciate the great personal sacrifice that has been made.

To the Oxford coach, Topolski, the selection decision was settled in a different way. He asked Clark to row on bowside, leaving Ward out of the crew and putting in McDonald. His decision caused a rift, as the crew Topolski suggested 'wasn't the fastest possible crew', the crew said. They demanded further trials. This demand was supported by a few of the coaches who became involved. However, there was some disagreement in deciding an appropriate means to test the difference between the oarsmen, and there was a strong feeling that any further trials would not be fair because the crew had already decided who they thought should take the last two places.

To solve the dilemma, several outside coaches were drafted in and asked to show their support to Topolski's decisions. The story they were told was that the dispute was about a selection decision between two individuals, not three; Ward was now firmly placed in the last bowside seat, and the selection decision they were asked to make was between Clark and McDonald for the last strokeside seat. Mike Spracklen, OBE, (chief coach of the National Men's team in Britain and part-time coach of Oxford for six years) was the only coach out of the nine called in to state quite clearly that Clark was the better oarsman of the two. Mark Lees (professional coach of The University of London Boat Club) abstained from supporting either oarsman, although he made it clear the the President's decision should stand, because that is how the Boat Race has always been run. The rest of the coaches and old Oxford Rowing Blues who had been called in voted in support of McDonald's selection over Clark's. The meeting which gave McDonald the majority also voted to drop Clark from the squad altogether, because they said he was a 'disruptive influence'.

In the space of four days, Chris Clark had gone from a position of being selectable for the last bowside seat in the first crew to not being allowed to even be considered for a position in the Boat Race second crew. The crew were outraged by the decision to ban Clark, and refused to row until things were changed. They demanded that Clark was reinstated in the Boat Club and that more trials be carried out. But things didn't change, and the crew became entangled in a bitter and embarrassing row with Topolski and McDonald. Communication between the two sides was limited, and as the row grew more intense and outside interest thickened, the two sides became more and more determined not to give in; the President wanted his crew back, but without Clark. The crew wanted more trials which were to include Clark on strokeside. To solve this dilemma, after weeks of uncomfortable indecision, the President pulled rank and, supported by the powers of the Boat Club Constitution and of the Dark Blue Establishment, dropped Clark from the crew altogether. His action and the display of power politics which led to this final decision was seen as sacrilegious by the other four

American Internationals, and, in support of sporting ethics which to them meant the fastest crew should race, they refused to row. Thus the fastest Boat Race crew on record never got a chance to race for Oxford; instead a slower crew rowed the race, compromising the very nature of the Boat Race excellence ethic, not to mention the tradition of fairness and honesty which the race is meant to represent.

To qualify to row in the Oxford Blue Boat and race in the Boat Race, you must be resident at Oxford as a student, either as an undergraduate or graduate. You must also be one of the best eight oarsmen resident at the University at that time. International and club standard oarsmen compete for a place in the boat, with the singular aim of beating Cambridge over one four-and-a-half mile race on the Thames Tideway in March. Many of rowing's great heroes have raced in the Boat Race, and they remember it well. For those stars who have never been to Oxford or Cambridge and thus, have never rowed the Boat Race, the attraction is there.

Steven Redgrave, twice Olympic and World gold medallist, speaks with a little despondency at never having had the chance to row the great race. He has worked his way through the full spectrum of rowing events, local regattas, National events and finally World and Olympic Championships, and he is now a household name. Individually he has done more to make rowing a recognised sport than any other oarsman in the country. Steven respects the Boat Race as an event which millions watch annually, and speaks fondly of the race which, he says, does a lot to raise the standard of oarsmen in this country. It is one of the only occasions when rowers of such differing standards will spend a whole season training and rowing together in the same crews, and thus for the club oarsmen, many of whom are trying to reach the dizzy heights of the National team, it is a chance to utilise the experience and skill of those who are better than them and to learn the finer points of rowing that distinguish medal winners from the also-rans.

In one year there may be up to eight internationals competing for a place in the Blue Boat, the number being determined by fate alone. Despite rumours of coaches finding places at the University for non-scholarly individuals who could help Oxford to win the Boat Race, the coaching team can do little but canvas oarsmen who are thinking of applying to study.

During recent years Oxford has been renowned for the larger number of Internationals in its crews, more so than Cambridge, and accusations have flown between the Universities about Oxford accepting students purely to boost its Boat Race crew. Steven Peel, Cambridge President during the 1987 Oxford dispute, embodied this feeling by announcing in *The Times* (29 January) 'that it was a problem of their own making'. Referring to the five American Internationals, he said, 'we feel it is bad for the Boat Race – it should be for genuine students. I am really not sure what these guys are doing here'. In fact there are many legitimate reasons that have nothing to do with rowing that make Oxford more likely to have more older and more international students available to row in the Boat Race. Oxford has more specific short courses aimed at attracting international graduates than Cambridge. It also has a scholarship grant available for international athletes who wish to study at Oxford. The nature of the Oxford postgraduate medical course is such that medics tend to come from Cambridge to Oxford, rather than the other way round.

Topolski did a lot to nourish the rumours of Oxford talent-grabbing: he could regularly be seen at International regattas touting for International oarsmen who were considering coming to England to study. With his charm and flamboyant personality, he was the perfect person to persuade such oarsmen to apply to Oxford rather than Cambridge. His methods were purely persuasive, as he had no power to gain entrance for non-academic oarsmen, but he could do a lot to point them in the right direction, give them the right contacts and enthuse them so that their application was fully committed.

Michael Barry, Senior Treasurer of the OUBC and a fellow of St. John's College, often receives primary applications from American and English oarsmen who want to study at Oxford. Because of his connection to the Boat Club, the coaches or president will often give his name to oarsmen who want to apply to study. However, during the dispute, Dr. Barry made his position on sporting qualification for a place at the University quite clear. 'I think that having the Americans is a good thing. People seem to think that they can came over to England and get let in because they can row. The Americans are all very good scholars who passed a stiff entrance procedure'. When oarsmen approach him, his role is to offer advice and guidance, not a back door. He makes it quite clear that there is no longer a place for the 'sporting jock' amongst the competitive academia of Oxford or Cambridge, and that tutors expect their students to maintain a high standard of work – Boat Race or not. In 1987, the Americans were all highly academically qualified, but their interest in their studies was scorned by McDonald and Topolski, who insisted that the Boat Race should be their first priority.

Each year the question of how many Internationals Oxford and Cambridge have on their crews is of great interest. Having a large number of skilful oarsmen and a good percentage of the previous year's squad is a good base upon which to build a winning Boat Race crew. Each year the coaching team wait with bated breath to discover how strong their squad will be. Managing this transient rowing population is part of the whole Boat Race excitement. Each year the system must adapt to attract the best oarsmen and give them what they need to perform to the best of their ability, whilst also maintaining a sense of continuity and status quo for the developing oarsmen who hopefully will eventually make up a part of our National team.

Top-class oarsmen, like other top-class athletes, are peculiar creatures, some easy to get along with and self-motivated, others difficult and often morose. They may need to be stroked or cajoled into performing at their very best. But because they are among the best, understanding and good management of their egocentricities is a job worth doing. At Oxford, to be prepared for a vast array of potential problems is the job of the chief coach and President of the Boat Club.

Daniel Topolski was the chief coach for Oxford for many years. He was responsible for the Oxford Boat Race successes from 1972 until his retirement after the 1987 Boat Race. During those years Oxford won twelve times, a change from the sixteen successive losses recorded in the years prior to his engagement. Oxford's wins under Topolski have received far more coverage and will be remembered more than Cambridge's sixteen successive wins because of Topolski himself. He is in every way a showman who thrives upon success and public image. Complementary to his desire for success, his arrival at Oxford as coach was recognised by his immediate desire for change. He instigated a whole new approach to training and coaching, making the training much harder and writing training programmes of such intensity that they would be punishing enough for oarsmen training to win the World Championships let alone the Boat Race.

He generated a coaching team of the very best coaches in the country; John Pilgrim-Morris, Richard Burnell and Steve Royle were brought in in the early days, and each year he added as much new coaching talent as he could. In short, he shook out the cobwebs and channelled some fighting spirit into the Oxford rowing boys. After a couple of years under Topolski's leadership, Oxford had their first win. Topolski, not satisfied with winning, urged the television to take an interest, and summoned the Press to liven up the Great University Challenge and to recognise Oxford and their new leader as the crew to back.

Topolski's tale is one of success. He did what he set out to do, and made Oxford the winning side. Keeping Oxford as the winning side was made easier by the constant influx of good oarsmen: success breeds success, and, as it had for Cambridge for sixteen years, it was now doing the same for Oxford. Oxford attracted the winning oarsmen and coaches, and thus the race stayed with them. With the winning streak and the renewed Press interest, Topolski became a media figure; he was the source of continuity that the punters could relate to, and he accepted his new image with an ease which would benefit Oxford tremendously.

Everybody likes to speculate who will win and the reasons why whichever crew continues to win year in and year out. For his reign as chief coach, Topolski became that reason: he was the Boat Race wizard. As Topolski's success continued, his own involvement became less and less. In some years he was noticeable only by his absence, until the last fortnight before the race, when once again he would don his coach's hat and add the finishing touches to an already polished crew.

Unfortunately, Topolski's career as an Oxford coach didn't have such a happy ending. At the end of 1987, the year of the great controversy, Oxford lost Topolski as chief coach. He was central to the whole dispute. It had been a trying year for Topolski, as the American Internationals in residence had brought their own ideas about how a Boat Race should be won, and, although prepared to listen to Topolski and his coaches when they arrived, they soon found that their English training partners seemed disillusioned with Topolski's very heavy and inefficient training regimes and his absence from coaching. Hence they were ready to accept advice from the Americans on how training should be done.

By 1987, Topolski was obviously fairly confident that his system of preparation for the race worked and would carry on working in his absence. Thus the amount of time he spent coaching was quite small and scattered. He was thus unaware of the brewing discontent amongst his oarsmen. On the odd occasion when he appeared, the oarsmen looked to him for advice and to answer their queries, but Topolski interpreted their queries as normal questioning. He sought mainly to avoid confrontation whenever he was questioned on a point of training or technique, and would seek to compromise or cajole them into forgetting the issue, as he had done in the past.

The unhappiness was more widespread than he was aware of; his lack of awareness about the individuals he was dealing with went a long way toward enhancing the lack of communication which ensued in the dispute, and not surprisingly Topolski found the challenges his rowers were making and the criticisms and questions difficult to handle. During the selection crisis, Topolski felt challenged and looked to the Oxford establishment to support him as his coaching had supported Oxford over the years. He was prepared to use arguments about the American failure to comply with his training programmes and the endless questioning of his system to back up and confuse the selection issue. He sided with the selection of McDonald over Clark, avoiding the Ward McDonald-Clark question totally, and he was prepared to dig out all the daily tussles which had occurred that season between coach and athletes, assuming the role of an established coach under personal attack to make sure that he and McDonald won the argument. Before the dispute, the whole squad had made their feelings clear about the training demands being placed upon them; these were harder than the programmes Topolski had produced before, and involved a lot of time-wasting, and meant shortening the amount of time on the water to enhance the quality. Their requests were quite simple and were based upon their combined years of experience of training themselves and the knowledge they had acquired from others; they certainly didn't want to cut the work or change everything. Their ideas would complement the current programme and cut out the endless complaints that the oarsmen had about the training being too inefficient and taking too long to complete.

Topolski mistook their ideas as a personal attack to his 'winning formula' and an attempt to undermine his authority, and used these arguments when the selection dispute arose. The selection dispute had no direct connection with any earlier disagreements, but it was used by Topolski and McDonald as evidence to suggest that the Americans were trying to take control of the Boat Club, although the handling of these earlier problems had contributed to the general disillusionment and unhappiness of the whole squad.

There is a right balance to be struck between old and new methods, and a carefully planned combination will help coaches and oarsmen to stay on the winning line. This, argued the Americans, was the balance they were trying to find. They had no idea at the time that Boat Race oarsmen had openly tried for years to modify the training demands set by Topolski, but because of his obstinacy they had ended up doing so without his knowledge. Despite several such attempts on the part of the oarsmen, in 1987 there was another failure to find the right balance of training time and training ideas with which everybody could cope and could perform to their best ability; this time it stayed in the open.

Normally in situations of such controversy, one would hope that there would be enough team work, commitment to the common goal and mutual respect to hold the group together. But, as is often the case, these criteria were not adequately dealt with, and a crisis ensued where oarsmen and coaches had little mutual respect. Thus, when the selection argument broke loose, there were no threads of respect holding the group together, and, thanks to the power of the Press and the Oxford Establishment, a simple argument rapidly degenerated into a full-scale war. To the Press and the public the story was portrayed as a nationalistic battle: US vs GB. Topolski and McDonald were portrayed as heroes protecting the University and the Boat Race from an unprecedented attempt by five US International oarsmen to seize control of the Oxford University Boat Club. The Great British Press have a lot to answer for in escalating the controversy: their morbid interest and biased reporting caused outrage amongst the oarsmen. At no stage throughout the dispute did they speak to the 'accused' Americans, nor did they reliably portray the British oarsmen's involvement. Instead, they followed a line of US versus GB which was both more glamorous and more likely to cause a stir than anything else they might care to write. How else the story flourished is difficult to understand, for if anyone had really stopped to think about this accusation, they might have realised that the idea of five US oarsmen of great repute trying to overthrow a boat club which would be theirs for just one year does seem a trifle bizarre! The American quest, along with the rest of the Blue Boat squad, was over fair selection, a fair chance to find the fastest crew, and some honesty and communication from the coaches that they were dealing with.

Potentially, they had a very fast crew, in which everybody wanted to row. If McDonald was the fourth man on strokeside, then Clark would either be out of a place or would row on bowside. However, if he then rowed on bowside, either Tony Ward or Hugh Pelham would lose their seat undeservedly, as they had both beaten Clark on bowside. The crew acknowledged Clark should be in the crew, but on strokeside. McDonald disagreed. Whichever way the dilemma is viewed, someone is to lose out. By the rules of sport, that man must be the slowest man. Finding the slowest man, or rather the eight fastest men by selection over races, ergometer tests and coaching discretion is a task which, if seen to be unfair by the oarsmen, will always be challenged. The extraordinary demands of training that are suffered to become a part of the best crew mean that the selection process should be such that the crew almost selects itself. If the best men do not end up in the crew, it makes a mockery of the whole system.

On the day of the race, without the five US Internationals aboard, the Oxford Blue Boat sported eight oarsmen and a cox all resilient to the hectic past two months. Those nine men had a mission to beat Cambridge and, despite predictions that they didn't have a hope, it was all credit to them that they did win, although some bad planning by the Cambridge coaches and a sickly Cambridge crew went a long way toward helping Oxford. The Cambridge crew remember the race as one that they lost, rather than the one that Oxford won. The Press shamefully reported the win as a personal victory for McDonald and a triumph over his enemy, not Cambridge, but the Oxford oarsmen who had challenged his right to row in the Blue Boat against Cambridge.

Personal vendetta is not what the Boat Race is about, nor ever should be. McDonald proved he was good enough to beat Cambridge, but still has to prove his worth against Clark or any other of the five Americans who, by right of being accepted to study at the University, should have had the right to row because they were all part of the elite that made up the fastest eight oarsmen in residence at the University in 1987.

The year following the dispute saw the instatement of Christopher Penny, one of the US oarsmen, as President for the 1988 Boat Race. During his reign he instituted changes to the Boat Race Constitution which would prevent any future President enforcing his will upon a crew without the entire support of his Boat Race squad. He also changed the training regime with the help of Mike Spracklen. His changes are still in use, and the oarsmen who row for Oxford nowadays are blissfully unaware of the disorganised chaos for which the Oxford Boat Club was known just a couple of years ago. Except, that is, for the last of the oarsmen who were rowing when Topolski was in control and are still rowing now. They are thankful for the changes that allow them more time to do other things whilst still completing a hefty but efficient training programme in preparation for the Boat Race, which has made Oxford the winning crew in 1988 and 1989, and now 1990, maintaining the winning sequence which began in 1972.

2

In 1986, the year before the dispute, Oxford lost the Boat Race by a staggering eight lengths; it was their first defeat for eleven years. To the coaches, the defeat didn't come as much of a surprise. Journalist Chris Dodd had quoted Oxford coach Mike Spracklen in *The Guardian* some weeks before the race, saying that if Cambridge didn't win this year, they never would! Spracklen was rather annoyed at Dodd for printing such home truths about the crew he was coaching, as Dodd's tactlessness did nothing for Oxford's confidence. 'All we could do was to train them to as high a standard as they were capable of reaching, and then hope something went wrong in the Cambridge crew who were obviously better than us,' Spracklen said.

There was little surprise at the defeat from any of the coaches; Topolski described his feeling on defeat as 'irritting rather than disappointing'. Disappointment is an emotion that accompanies broken expectation, and for Topolski the expectation was that his crew would lose, his irritation being founded in not being able to ward off the inevitable defeat. That year Cambridge had acquired some of the talent that Oxford had previously been infamous for. On board they had two current British Internationals, Steve Peel from the GB Coxless Four, Paddy Broughton from the GB Eight, and six others all verging on making it into the National team. Their strength was in the similarity of their talent, competition between individuals for a place in the Blue Boat was strong, and, once together, the crew was strengthened by their combined trust in each other. In comparison the Oxford crew was made up of two American Internationals, one unfit Australian International and five other oarsmen of no particular repute. It had been hard to scrape together eight men of 'Blue Boat'.

In a year like this, there is little doubt who is likely to win. The Boat Race, like any other race, goes to the fastest crew and, contrary to myth, it is a race which tends to run to form, the 1986 being no exception. In the run up to the Boat Race, both Oxford and Cambridge traditionally race a number of races against crews such as the University of London crew, the National Eight and other Tideway-trained crews. The races serve as preparation for the big race, and also as a good indicator of the relative speeds of the two crews. That year, the Cambridge crew were regularly demonstrating their superiority over the less impressive Oxford eight. In those pre-races, Cambridge had beaten Oxford convincingly in the Reading Fours Head at the start of the winter, then, once formed into Eights, they raced the 'Tideway-wise' University of London Eight and beat them. Just two weeks later, Oxford suffered a defeat against the same crew. Cambridge also raced the GB National Eight, suffering a narrow defeat against the same crew that had made mincemeat of the Oxford Eight just a week earlier. There seemed no doubt that, for the first time in eleven years, Cambridge were going to win the Boat Race. The only thing that could save Oxford now was one of the freak happenings which the public love to witness and remember about the Boat Race, like the years when one or other crew sinks in the especially rough conditions. Cambridge were the first to go down, as long ago as 1859. Oxford could do with another such happening this year; it was the only thing likely to save the race for them.

Topolski recognised his crew was outclassed, and searched in desperation to boost the crew's speed. Graham Jones, an Australian World medallist, ex-Oxford President and Blue several times over, seemed the obvious answer. He had declined an invitation to row in the boat until just two weeks before the Race. He had been a part of the Boat Race training early in Michaelmas term, but had dropped out quite early in the term, having decided to dedicate his time to finishing his thesis. His late addition to the crew was a desperate attempt to utilise all rowing power present on

Oxford turf. Sadly, Jones alone could not make up for the comparative lack of power, experience and talent in the Oxford boat.

Topolski's irritation at not being able to produce a winning crew showed. Known for his undying determination to win at all costs, his reshuffling of the crew was inevitable, if not greatly appreciated by his crew. Despite such efforts, Oxford still lost the race. In losing, Topolski lost more than a Boat Race, he also lost the respect of the Oxford crew who had invested a high degree of trust and respect in him, the kind of respect that winning had nurtured over ten years and the kind of respect he would undoubtedly need for the next year, particularly as his method of coaching relies so much on a lot of trust being divested in him as a coach.

His coaching is based upon demand. He demands of his oarsmen as much as they can physically take, pushing them to their limits in training every day, in a 'do as I say and you will win' approach. His personal drive and determination rubs off on his young apprentices such that they will find themselves racing and training harder than they thought was possible, but it is a gutsy, cold-blooded approach with little finesse, and it has one shortfall which the 1986 crew became party to. They invested their belief in Topolski's philosophy that if you train hard enough and push yourself far enough you will win, which is fine until you race a superior crew. Then, no matter how hard they pushed, they could not win. They invested their energy in the regime but it didn't work, and when they lost the Boat Race they lost confidence in their own abilities, and in the coaching system, too. Whatever the reason given to them for losing, the question which will stick in their minds is 'Did I push myself hard enough?', the answer being no, because if they had they would have won. The next question is 'Can I pull any harder?', and the answer may be filled with self-doubt. These sorts of questions prey on any athlete's mind, but if they are allowed to become foremost in the mind then they can be detrimental to performance.

Training is all about pushing back barriers and pushing yourself to the limit in preparation for a competition. Top athletes and coaches realise the importance of knowing your own capabilities and carefully planning progress forward so that irrationalities like constantly questioning your own ability are never allowed to affect performance. Losing a race must be carefully explained, and a method to combat the loss carefully worked out. Topolski's way of combating the loss in 1986 was to seek more hours on the water, more training and more fitness with his 1987 crew, but they didn't respect fitness as the reason why they lost, and certain members of the squad, Clark in particular, were guarded about Topolski's methods, and were prepared to speak out. Topolski later said that the price you pay for losing was that people start to think you need to change; he was no exception, he wanted change, but he obviously felt that the way things needed to change was by doing more training, and he sought no other new methods.

Topolski, Clark and McDonald returned in 1987, each to prove his worth and each desperate to put Oxford back on the winner's pedestal. Unfortunately for Topolski each returned with his own opinions on how to go about winning the 1987 Boat Race, and on why they had lost in 1986. Topolski convinced himself something avoidable had been wrong all year, and in looking for an answer to this feeling his thoughts turned wrongly to the only person in the squad who he had been unable to get close to, Chris Clark. Topolski openly laid blame for the eight length defeat upon Christopher Clark, the six man in the Blue Boat, who, Topolski said, 'stopped pulling in the middle of the race'. His justification for this personal attack is difficult to explain; one man does not make a crew lose by such a big margin. It is much more likely, as Spracklen surmised at the coaches' meeting following the race, that the Oxford crew were in reality two or three lengths slower than Cambridge. 'Cambridge caught them and passed them and towards the end of the race some people lost heart and stopped pulling to their maximum, which left them eight lengths behind, and not two or three'. Clark was one of those men. Only winning mattered to Clark, not how far they lost by. Spracklen wasn't admonishing Clark's action, but explained to me that if the six man, a key position in the boat, is much better than the majority of the crew, then he will fight to win but must also fight to hold the crew together, a very difficult thing to do. 'Clark's mentality is such that in certain circumstances he will lose hope'. He had lost hope in that race when he could no longer see in himself the power to hold the crew together. Clark did not lose the 1986 Boat Race singlehandedly: there were eight men in the crew, and eight men lost that race to eight better oarsmen from Cambridge. It is important never to attribute a loss to one athlete; an Eight must be seen as a crew. Singling out one individual as a culprit is as good as writing them off for good, and will do nothing to instil the important bond of trust which must exist between coach and athlete. When a crew loses, carefully assessing and discussing each man's deficiencies will motivate each individual to concentrate on eliminating those deficiencies. But Topolski needed an explanation, and Clark, who had challenged his training regime and his psychology, provided the explanation he was looking for.

Topolski revels in the stories of the monumental Herculeses who had through history held the Oxford oar handles and toiled senselessly through hours and hours of physical abuse in an effort to make their Blue Boat beat Cambridge. Clark didn't fit this maxim. But he was determined that his new squad, Clark included, would. Topolski returned determined to reinstate his authority, demanding more training, more fight and more cunning. For McDonald, now President, the job was to lead the way and make sure nobody was allowed to slacken, and that everybody's skills were developed to their best.

Clark returned adamant to help Oxford to victory. The previous year had been difficult for Clark: he had found training with Topolski's programmes and with oarsmen not as good as himself harder and much more demoralising than he had expected. It was a lot different to the quality and perfection of national squad training he had been used to in the States. He had really wanted to win that Boat Race, but perhaps more than the rest of the crew, he had been painfully aware that the Oxford crew was not good enough for them to win. As the best man in the crew, his role in 1986 was to lead them and teach them whatever he could and, along with his partner George Livingstone, he did his best to lead from the front, something which neither of them had been used to. Back at home in the trials and training camps of the US national squad, both of them assumed the positions of being not as good as the established members of the team, and they were happy to learn from anyone who would help them. In Oxford, the tables were turned and, being the best, it was their job to try to help, offer advice and lead by example.

Clark remembers feeling enthusiastic but unsure about his ability to impart enough knowledge to shape the crew into a winning one. He recollected to me his feeling of helplessness as the race drew near. Being one of the best in the crew, he felt responsible for making the crew perform well enough to beat Cambridge. Clark is the sort of person to shoulder personal blame, and he felt responsible for not being able to teach the crew enough to make them win. Winning that race meant everything to him. His disappointment at losing the race was personal, and he was determined not to lose next year. His determination to not let it happen again was channelled into trying to change the parts of the training and preparation that he thought were wrong and wasteful of time and effort.

Clark returned in 1987 determined to win the race, and, in short, he didn't trust Topolski to help Oxford do that. He wanted to cut the hours and hours of fruitless land training and weightlifting, and, instil a sense of integrity into the work on the water; at bottom, he wanted to change the training regimes that represented Topolski and his Boat Race ethic. Clark thought his ideas were obvious improvements, and couldn't see why they hadn't been integrated before. He had only a year left at Oxford, and less than that to prepare for the next race, and his urgency in trying to make people see what he was trying to say was clear. He believed that Topolski would trust in his ideas about training, and that things would be different in 1987. This naive belief was typical of this enthusiastic but slightly arrogant young oarsman.

When he returned, things weren't noticeably different. The only real difference was that Topolski wanted MORE training. Clark was astounded; it was a major blow to his ideas. There was a fundamental difference between Clark's ideas and Topolski's, and they both failed to communicate that difference. Topolski didn't want to listen, and Clark found that frustrating. 'Quite frankly,' he told me, 'I thought it would be better if he wasn't asked to be head coach, and I wasn't scared to say so. With a new President and a new squad, there is the opportunity to change things, and I thought it would be easier to change coach than change the way he ran things, because Topolski thought his way was best.'

Topolski gave out training programmes and made it clear he didn't want to change anything. Clark was quick to suggest that Topolski's programme should be changed from the start; he was anxious to get the year sorted out. He warned the other Americans that things needed to change, but his warnings were ignored. The rest of the squad were intially reluctant to disrupt and question the Oxford coaching system: 'They felt that they couldn't commit themselves to back a decision to ask another coach to take over. They didn't feel they had the right, and I guess that was true.'

The reluctance of the rest of the rowers to push for change left Clark smouldering. He was in a difficult position. His friends weren't prepared to accept what he told them about the training schedules and chaos that he had experienced the previous year, because they were exercising the natural caution which goes with entering a new environment. Clark was prepared to challenge Topolski's leadership because he really wanted to win the Boat Race; he appreciated Topolski's reputation, but felt the great man had lost sight of what he was doing. He took a lot of criticism from his friends for his 'attitude'; nobody likes militants, even though throughout history it is often militant thought which had progressed the Boat Race forward in its training and technique: Rod Carnegie, from Melbourne University, President of the OUBC in 1957, initiated revolutionary training. He took his ideas from Harry Hopman and Frank Stampfl and, although seen as 'troublesome and revolutionary' at the time, his efforts paid off. He didn't want to overthrow college rowing, but he wanted speed and stamina, and he set about coaching it. He attributed his ability to make changes to being a foreigner. It didn't make it easy, but he thought that if he had been to an English public school he would not have been able or felt the desire to make changes. Clark, too, wanted to make changes, but he needed the support of others to do it, and needed their confidence. They were soon to realise that they should have listened to Clark. In retrospect, it is not surprising that the year took a turn for the worse.

All started well. Fresh from a summer vacation, the core of the 1987 Boat Race squad could be seen powering up and down the Isis, carrying out a somewhat chaotic training schedule of hard rowing designed to induce the sort of fitness required of Boat Race oarsmen. The majority of the group, Donald McDonald, Tony Ward, Tom Cadoux-Hudson, Gavin Stewart, Hugh Pelham, Paul Gleeson and Mathew Ridgewell had been a part of the 1986 Boat Race squad. They had slightly less than seven months to prepare for the race, but for the oarsmen with a winter of hard training ahead, the race seemed a lifetime away. With the three Internationals and the enthusiasm and dedication of the rest of the group, they looked to build a promising crew which would hopefully put Oxford back on the winner's pedestal after the embarassing defeat in 1986. The squad were keen to get started, well aware that Cambridge had retained some of their last year's winning crew; they would be a tough lot to beat.

The core of the group was an enthusiastic bunch and, spurred on by the thought of winning their Blues, they had returned to Oxford early to prepare for the Pairs Head of the River Race. The race would be just a bit of fun for the oarsmen, but used wisely would get soft summer vacation bodies back on the road to fitness. Every man was anxious to get an early lead on the 'filth from the Fens' and to secure his seat in this year's Oxford Blue Boat. However, unknown to this group of athletes, Chris, Tom and Rob were not the only international calibre oarsmen to grace the Oxford waters this year. There were four other internationals who had places at Oxford that year, and they would soon be joining the rest in the quest to win the Boat Race. The four were Americans, three rowers and a cox, all World medallists. Their appearance *en masse* was little more than a coincidence; they had all come to Oxford to study and hopefully to become a part of the celebrated

Oxbridge tradition, the Boat Race. With them they brought an impressive list of rowing and academic qualifications: Chris Penney had been an Olympic silver medallist in 1984 and bronze medallist in 1985. He had come to Oxford to study for an M.Phil in History at St. John's College. Dan Lyons, gold medallist in the US Four in 1986, had joined Oriel College to read for a Social Studies diploma with the hope of later converting to an M.Phil in History. Jon Fish and Chris Huntington had both come to read for a Social Studies diploma at Mansfield College: Jon had coxed Penney and Huntington to a bronze medal in 1985 in the Eight, and Huntington in the bronze-winning Coxed Four in 1986. With their arrival came every Boat Race President's dream, and McDonald's was no exception. He was well aware that having six senior world medallists aboard a Boat Race crew which would normally contain no more than two or three oarsmen of such a high standard was certainly one recipe for winning the race. Having lost in 1986, to be President of a winning crew that year was his one and only goal.

McDonald's Boat Race squad remember the arrival of the Americans with little enthusiasm. Tony Ward recounts the day when he met Chris Clark with Chris Penney in Oriel Square. Clark introduced Penney and his credentials with the news that Huntington, Lyons and Fish would be arriving soon. 'It was quite a shock, because it was the first I knew about there being five Americans coming to study at Oxford that year. Normally I would've expected to hear via the grapevine or from the President if there were to be any 'stars' rowing in the race.' Tony wasn't the only one to find the news a bit of a shock: the whole squad was fairly disturbed by it. On the one hand it was good news because, barring disaster, Oxford would almost certainly win the Boat Race. However, they were jolted by the realisation that with five Internationals in the squad, there were only three places in the 1987 Blue Boat left for them to fight for, and everyone was going to be training to make sure that one of those three places was theirs. Between them, Cadoux-Hudson, Lyons, Penney, Clark and Huntington had countless years more rowing experience than the whole of the rest of the 1986 Boat Race squad, and much of that experience had been gained at world class level; their talent and experience was indisputable. To get to the top they all would have been through years of hard training, both on the water and in the gym; they would have had to prove their individual ability against some of the best in the world, they would have proven their ability to adapt to rowing in different crews as well, and they would have experienced the pressures of public and press attention which you meet as a successful athlete; in short, they had all the qualities which most of the others were still trying to develop. For the squad, the year had taken on a whole new perspective. One thing seemed certain: Oxford would win the Boat Race; but which of the non-Internationals would make up the numbers in which was likely to be the fastest Boat Race crew on record?

Both President and coach are normally excited about the arrival of Internationals to boost the team and would tell the squad early on, as everybody should be excited about extra power and skill. By not telling the boys, Topolski and McDonald unknowingly created an air of deceit. It wasn't a feeling unknown to this particular bunch of oarsmen, as the previous year the late selection of Graham Jones, an Australian who had supposedly dropped out of the Boat Race, had created the same kind of uneasiness amongst their teammates. Not knowing the score is something athletes hate most of all.

The saga in 1986 started when Graham Jones, who had dropped out of the Boat Race to work for his Ph.D was reinstated into the Blue Boat very late in the day. Tony Ward was the oarsman who lost his seat to Jones in the 1986 crew. Graham stood in the class of international oarsmen that, when fit and willing, are an invaluable asset. Because of his proven ability, several attempts had been made to get him to return to the crew earlier on in the year, but his refusal was definite; he needed, he said, to spend the time working for his Ph.D, and therefore couldn't really complete the training demands made upon a Boat Race oarsman, particularly not in the Boat Club's present state of disorganisation. As the season progressed, rumours were heard by the crews that Topolski was still trying to coax Jones into returning to row. The oarsmen asked Topolski if the rumours were true, and were reassured that this wasn't the case. His reappearance therefore, in late February, unfit but keen to save Oxford from the defeat which Topolski was predicting, demonstrated that in fact Topolski had lied and had never given up trying to reach Jones. This deception may seem trivial, particularly to non-athletes, but to the oarsmen concerned there was no doubt of the seriousness of this 'offence'. In a system where only the best man wins, there is a certain importance in clarity which is hard to explain. To the oarsmen, Jones's unscheduled return meant that one of them was to lose his seat; a seat which had he had trained hard for and made sacrifices for in his University life, sacrifices he was glad to make in a system of fair play. But the selection of Jones wasn't seen to be fair play; he wasn't trialled and he also wasn't fit: his unquestioned selection and Topolski's faith in him wasn't enough to reassure the crew that he should be in with them, especially as he apparently made the crew more uncomfortable and not noticeably faster. There is no doubt that in sport there is an expectation of fair play, an expectation that all the cards will be laid on the table. There will always be disagreements and heartache when individuals are pushed to their absolute limits, but the job of a good coach and manager revolves around making selection obvious and dealing with disappointments as tactfully as possible. Jones's late selection wasn't introduced tactfully, nor was it fair play by the time he arrived, as the Blue Boat had already been announced, and Graham Jones forgotten.

Tony Ward found this sort of deception unacceptable because there were individuals in that crew whose rowing and academic careers both were coming to an end that year; choosing to row in the Boat Race had meant sacrificing, to a certain extent, their academic results. If Jones had stayed on the team as a fit International, he almost certainly would have been in the crew, and some of the others might not have chosen to sacrifice academia, having calculated that they would be the ones to be selected last. Rowing in the Boat Race is important, but so is doing well academically. Topolski's training demands made it difficult to fully dedicate enough time to both aspects of your life, because rowing took up so much time. For those in their final year who look like not quite making the first crew, there is an important decision to be made after Christmas: whether to continue investing their time in the Boat Race or their studies.

When Jones was brought back, Ward stepped down from his place in the 1986 Boat Race crew, partly he says, from disgust at such a deception, and partly because it was his first year at Oxford and therefore he would have the chance to row in the Boat Race again, whereas the other likely candidate to be replaced by Jones was in his last year. By standing down, Ward made a moral stand which the rest of the squad respected, and also a gesture which many felt should never have been necessary. Topolski, it seems, lost a lot of face with that crew for his decision to put Jones in the boat.

The unannounced arrival of four International oarsmen and a cox was a distrubing reminder of the previous year's misgivings, and was to be the first step in fuelling the distrust and deceit between coaches and oarsmen which, by the time the uncomfortable process of selection started in earnest, was rife in the squad.

The initial misgivings the squad had about the American involvement in the Boat Race were soon dispelled by the infectious enthusiasm for rowing, the Boat Race and Oxford University life which all four Americans possessed in abundance. The parts that these individials were to play were of mentor and technician, not only to the Boat Race boys but also to the hundreds of other students who enjoy rowing at Oxford in the numerous college races. They were keen to impart their expertise to a system of rowing which produces half of the women's National squad and about a third of the potential oarsmen for the men's team. Penney and Fish in particular could often be seen cycling up and down the banks of the river Isis, offering their expert advice to the novice college oarsmen and women. They soon found themselves coaching the Boat Race rowers as well, both when they were rowing together and when on dry land. Gavin Stewart remembers, 'They were real technicians; when we rowed they searched for perfection in their bladework, and they taught us to do the same. They spent a lot of time with some of the less technically good oarsmen, just teaching them the skill involved in good rowing. It was a new experience for a lot of us, because for the most we'd been taught rowing by Topolski, and the emphasis had been on hard work and the will to win. They taught us that you don't win races just by brute force. I owe a lot to them, my rowing technique improved enormously whilst they were here.'

Topolski was impressed with them, too. Hull remembers how, during their December training, Topolski couldn't stop telling them how tremendous the effort on the water was. 'He wasn't used to that sort of quality, and nor were we.' What Topolski saw and congratulated was a direct result of having Internationals on board, particularly in such large numbers: their experience and skill quickly starts to benefit the whole squad. International athletes are highly thought of throughout the world. Irrespective of country, colour or creed, an individual announced to have represented their country in a sport and who has achieved medallist standard will be treated with a certain amount of awe and respect. Everyone knows of the time and dedication it takes to reach the top in any sphere, and for those that make it, they will became a breed apart. Wherever they go they will receive a warm welcome and an overpowering curiosity which may mean that they will spend their spare time talking about their sport to audiences clamouring for their attention.

The Americans had imagined that rowing at Oxford would be no different to rowing anywhere else in the world. Huntington, Fish and Lyons had thought it would be a great place to train and study the year before Olympic year in preparation for the Games, whilst also gaining from the international experience, and for Penney, who had retired from the International team, it would be a satisfying way to end his rowing career. Their dreams and their expectations had been led astray, and they soon found out, as Clark had warned them, that training at Oxford was perhaps not such a good way to build for the Olympics. There was so much that was great about Oxford rowing, they loved the college rowing and the widespread enthusiasm that filled the colleges near to college race times, but the Boat Race training was not quite what they had imagined. They soon found themselves involved in a system of organised chaos, where the training was not nearly as advanced in its technique as they were used to.

The established squad, which had been in training for over a month, had talked endlessly about their rowing goals for the year, how they were going to beat Cambridge, and even who was to sit in which seat in the Blue Boat that year. When the Americans arrived unannounced, all that was changed, and suddenly the enthusiasm and verve for training was challenged by a need for complete reassessment. 'We knew that some of us wouldn't make the boat now, because they were better than us. We felt cheated because neither Dan or Donald had warned us; it set us all off on the wrong footing.' Tony's thoughts set the scene for the months to follow. It wasn't a feeling of resentment of the Americans, but a serious feeling of distrust and uneasiness in President McDonald and coach Topolski. The squad needed some leadership, and they got it from the Americans, not from the President or from Topolski, who was only available to coach maybe once a week, sometimes less. Having the Americans was an asset, but it also meant that goals and training needed to be put in a slightly different perspective.

As for the Americans, they slotted into the Oxford rowing scene with relative ease. Only Clark remained sceptical, but then he'd seen it all before and was keen to see things changed for the better. Despite his misgivings, on his return to Oxford that winter, he too did his bit for college rowing and, with the ease of a likeable guy, could be seen coaching and rowing with almost anyone who asked him. The Americans became special to their colleges, as one would expect; Chris Penney could be seen at St. John's pulling the Second crew up and down the Isis with a pained, yet stoical expression on his face, determined to impart a small amount of his world-class knowledge to the keen but, for the most part, talentless crew. Lyons was able to row for Oriel College, strengthening an already good crew and Huntington and Fish did a lot for the rowing reputation of Mansfield College, a college which remains to this day not particularly renowned for its expertise with the oar!

Anyone who knew them knew their support and dedication to the sport and the development of the goldmine of oarsmen and women at Oxford. Enthusiasm was the name of the game, but they weren't there just to enjoy the Oxford tradition of rowing for fun, because for them rowing was a way of life. They had come to Oxford to study and to win the Boat Race. They rowed for their colleges because they loved the tradition and the events, and they wanted to put something back into the Oxford which was giving them so much pleasure. 'Frankly, we were amazed at how badly the colleges taught themselves to row! We thought it would be great to help them get away from the grandmaster thuggery that exists in Oxford college and Boat Race rowing. It was an ambitious aim,' recalls Fish. 'But when I first saw the rows and rows of college boathouses and the endless stream of oarsmen which blocked the Isis, I couldn't believe that Britain wasn't the best country in the world in the sport of rowing. I had never seen so many people rowing and wanting to row. The way people tried to teach each other, the lack of professionalism and the blood and guts that went with the rowing was chaotic, and I'd never seen anything like that either!'

The confusion they saw in the college rowing unfortunately spilled over into their own rowing for the Boat Race. Clark, the Evans twins, and many other Americans who had raced in the Boat Race before them, had warned them all of the long, long enduring hours they would spend on the water and in the gym, of Topolski's enthusiasm for 'more work', and of the wasted hours waiting for boats or oarsmen or coaches to arrive, all in the drizzly, cold English weather, but of course they hadn't believed it could be as bad as rumour suggested. After all, it was the Boat Race they were talking of, and everyone knows what a great race it is.

Thus, for the Americans the year started with a mixture of enchantment and wonder. They couldn't help but dive into Oxford life and Oxford rowing, wanting very much to become part of it. At the same time, they knew there were so many ways that things could be changed for the better. Impatient for the development of the Boat Race crew, they unknowingly set about instigating those changes, unprepared for the next four months of public and Oxbridge abuse that were to result from their natural enthusiasm and implicit belief in producing the fastest possible crew.

3

Organisation in the Oxford Boat Club had always been fairly chaotic, and how to cure the chaos had been a favourite topic for discussion for several years, particularly amongst visiting American oarsmen. Many of them having trained and rowed at their American colleges under full-time coaches and student managers, whose responsibility was the efficient functioning of the club, could see more efficient ways to run things than perhaps was immediately obvious. For example, when Chris Penney became President the following year, he applied some of the ideas learnt from American boat clubs to aid the running of OUBC, and began to create a sense of order within the club. His job was made easier because his Presidency coincided with the new sponsorship from Beefeater Gin, some of which was invested in a full-time administrator. Oxford was at last to join ranks with the many other University and College boat clubs who realised the necessity of paying a professional to organise their equipment and their oarsmen. Employing full-time coaches is something American University boat clubs have done for many years. (Harvard employed their first full-time professional coach/administrator in 1905.) Oxford, rather behind the times, has left the running of its Boat Club to the club President, his committee and chief coach.

Topolski donated his time as chief coach for the love of the sport. Over the last few years of his appointment, the significant sponsorship by Ladbrokes and then Beefeater meant that his dedication was boosted by a fee of £5,000 plus expenses, not enough to live on, but more than is received by the many coaches who generously donate their time and skill free of charge to the Boat Club.

Topolski's lack of financial support obviously meant that his ties to the Boat Club were purely personal, and he was in no way financially obligated to the Boat Race. He was very much his own boss, and thus had the freedom to come and go at his own will, coaching on days when it suited his timetable and, by all accounts, that was the way he liked it. As chief coach, Topolski would be just one of the coaches who would be involved with producing the Oxford crews. The system worked by having a pool of coaches, who would all donate their time free of charge. Each coach would cover the squad for about two weeks at a time, coaching as many sessions as they could. In the early half of the year, the crews would be coached for no more than two or three times in the week, and the other outings would be completed alone or as training in the gym. Topolski would coach most weekends, either alongside the coach for the week, or on his own. Once the crews had been selected, they would receive coaching in two-week periods, following a rota which had stayed fairly fixed for a few years.

The six week period leading up to the race, when the crews had been selected, was described by Spracklen as 'by chance, a fairly successful six weeks', mainly because three coaches, Royle, Spracklen and Topolski all had their own particular quirks, very different but complementary. Steve Royle would take the Blue Boat for the first two weeks. Steve is excellent at getting the crews to work hard and drive together, so that by the time they came to the second two-week stint with Mike Spracklen, they would be working hard as a crew, but their technical deficiencies would be beginning to show. Mike is a technical genius, and his two weeks would be spent ironing out some of the major faults in the crew, in the hope of creating a smooth, efficient Eight. The final two weeks would be spent based on the Tideway, the race venue, where Topolski, 'the finishing coach', would give them the race sparkle and enthusiasm that a winning crew would need. The combination of the coaches' talents worked well, and although they never talked between themselves about their plan of attack, in each two-week stint, it was evident that things would follow this particular route. Unfortunately, these six weeks were not representive of the rest of the year. In the early winter there would be a stream of coaches and helpers who would donate their time to the rowers, but, without any combined effort from the coaches to agree on a distinct style of rowing and training, there was a grave problem of discontinuity in the coaching. There was no-one to take the responsibility for answering questions about technical problems.

To the Americans, this was an obvious fault, and one which they broached several times with Topolski and McDonald. In his book, *Boatrace Revival*, Topolski points out the problems of coaches not agreeing on technical points. "But that's the opposite of what I was told last week" is one of the rowers' most common frustrations', Topolski quite rightly pointed out. Huntington said that they all felt sure that if they pointed out to Topolski that they were receiving conflicting advice they would be able to sit down and work out a technique that they all agreed on. The problem could be simple to solve if they could agree with all the coaches what they were aiming at, and also if possible to appoint someone to oversee problems like this and check that all the coaches, no matter how short a time they coached for, were aware of the policy. It was a simple idea, and would introduce a sense of continuity. The policy of having a full-time co-ordinator at the American boat clubs meant that Huntington, Lyons, Clark, Fish and Penney were used to this kind of professional communication, and they saw no problem in introducing it in Oxford.

The advent of a professional coaching position in 1988 was still unknown to most of the OUBC, but would definitely benefit the club in terms of continuity. The club would be able to take on a policy, such as agreeing on a technique and making sure all the coaching staff were aware of it, and there would be someone to administer the policy and spread the word. It was important organisational issues which the club lacked, and these would directly affect the performance of the rowers. The President alone didn't have the time to provide a support system such as this, nor could he be guaranteed to have the necessary skills or knowledge to perform this type of job well.

After his tremendous success with the Boat Race,

Topolski would obviously be offered first refusal on the co-ordinator/coaching job. There were some people who doubted his suitability to the job, himself included, and there was little doubt that there would be plenty of competition. To be the coach of a successful Boat Race squad is a very prestigious position. For the coach, the lures are very much the same as for the oarsman; it is one of the only times when the coach of an 'amateur' sport will receive a lot of publicity, and it is a chance to have a major effect on the development of young rowers in Britain, as well as being great fun. Steven Royle, long time Oxford coach and friend of Topolski's, was the other main contender for the new position. It is difficult to ascertain whether Royle was in fact given the job over Topolski or whether, after Topolski's resignation, he was the obvious candidate. Whatever the reasons, the job was eventually given to Royle.

The introduction of paid employees for the Boat Race was a dream of many old Blues, and Topolski was no exception. He had a lot to do with creating the ideas and structure for the development of the club, but he obviously had some reservations about his own involvement with the emergence of this structure. Well before the dispute, Topolski had talked to Spracklen about his feelings about being professionally employed by the Boat Club, and Spracklen remembers Topolski's insecurity about being involved in a more structured Boat Race environment; it seems this wasn't the way Topolski worked. The rumours of Topolski's retirement from the Boat Race were ghosting around the Oxford spires before the loss of '86, and, with the instigation of a professional set-up, it seemed as if those rumours were to be fulfilled.

The new changes would give the President more freedom to be able to concentrate on training. He would worry less about the day-to-day management of the equipment; jobs like moving boats from venue to venue, sorting out who was to coach when, and organising the storage and repair of the equipment. In short, Oxford was about to reorganise an out-of-date system which relied entirely on the President's desire for the maintenance of order. The problems which faced the President and the oarsmen were mainly to do with man and equipment management, and after a hard day's training it was all too easy for the odd boat to get left off a packed trailer, 'to be picked up later', or for the boats to be left on the trailer to be put away 'tomorrow', and for details of training or coaches' thoughts not to be passed on. Nobody quite knew who held overall responsibility for decisions to be made about when a boat needed repair, or who should make sure that all the oarsmen knew exactly where the outing was today, and who exactly was required for which crew and when, or even who had the copy of the training programme, and would make sure that the coach knew what work should be done. The threads of continuity were left to the President and the coaches who should have been donating their valuable time to rowing and coaching, and not to organising the day-to-day running of the club. Picked for his rowing talent, not his organisational skills, there is no guarantee, even with a lot of goodwill, that the President will be a good communicator or organiser.

The results of the system were twofold: firstly the Oxford boys carried with them the reputation of being a straggly lot who frequently couldn't even account for where their boats had been left. James Svenson-Taylor, from Ayling's Racing Boats, tells some raucous stories of the all-too-often Presidential telephone call: 'Ah, James, it's President X from Oxford, have you finished that four we left with you last year? We need it tomorrow!', or quite often the embarrassed question: 'Do you have our third eight in your workshop, we seem to have...err...lost it, and we wondered if we'd dropped it with you for repairs?' Evidence suggests that the problem wasn't disregard, but there was a serious lack of energy or ability on the President's behalf to organise a bunch of frivolous young men at the end of a day's training. The second problem was that, because of the chaos and manic atmosphere that surrounded the Oxford squad training, for many years visiting Internationals had tended to thrust aside Topolski's winter training programmes and set about training in a more efficient, 'what they were used to' way, usually without any detrimental effect. The Evans twins from Canada, Mark and Mike, were a perfect example of this. They rowed for Oxford together in 1983 and 1984, but spent much of their time training alone in a pair, following a programme which they considered was the training that would get them to their peak. They obviously were successful, as later, in 1984, they went on to win the Gold in the US Eight. Clark, too trained in 1986 for the most part in a pair with George Livingstone, content to do more work on the water, not bothering with senseless gym sessions.

Topolski never objected to this approach, probably because he didn't really know or care to ask; he trusted his Internationals to do their stuff. They didn't challenge him, so he wouldn't challenge them. It was skilful management on Topolski's part. If the younger, less experienced oarsmen had gone and done their own thing they wouldn't improve and wouldn't make the grade, but Internationals are driven by the desire to succeed: success and winning are ingrained in their way of life. However, having current Internationals ignoring the set programme would almost certainly eventually lead the rest of the squad to wonder at the usefulness of the programme. It was a demonstration that there were better ways to train, because the best generally know what's good for them, and they have spent a long time working it out. In 1987, with five individuals going their own way, the question of who was right soon arose, as leadership and advice were closer to hand from the other rowers than from the coaching team, because they spent a lot of time together. It was obviously more natural to seek advice from oarsmen of a better standard, thus giving the Americans a leadership role. McDonald, although President, didn't have the knowhow or experience that the Americans had. When questions arose about training or technique, their expert advice was sought. McDonald had a difficult job to lead these men, and was probably the wrong man to do it; he tried to lead from the front by training hard and showing uncompromising commitment, but his extra efforts still left him short of experience.

In the 1986 crew, Clark produced the top scores on the ergometer tests and was easily recognisable as the best oarsman on the water. He had trained away from the squad for most of the year, but had stayed at the top. Topolski was obviously impressed by his demonstrable ability to train himself effectively, and asked Clark if he would like to be President in 1987. Not wanting the commitment, Clark declined the offer; he was not the sort of person to want to be President. In the position of President some see honour and power and leadership; Clark saw hassle and distraction, for him the honour of being successful in the Boat Race was enough.

The only other Blue who would be returning in 1987 was McDonald, and he was duly made President. Elected by old Blues who are in residence in Oxford, and the College Boat Club Captains, the election is normally a formality. The coach and President generally agree on the best person to do the job, and if the rest of the crew agree, then that person is nominated and usually elected unchallenged.

McDonald wanted to be President, and was prepared to commit a lot of time to the running of the Boat Club, especially as this year he wanted to win the Boat Race. He had been Boat Club Secretary to President Bruce Philp in '86. Philp was possibly one of the most disorganised Presidents that the club had ever experienced: his unruly reputation ran the length of the University. A medical student in his final year, his time was much in demand and, combined with the Presidency, Bruce was a busy man. But for Bruce, obviously a popular character, one Presidency and a medical career wasn't enough, so, when asked, he also took on the position of Oxford Blues Committee President. The Blues Committee is an organization dedicated to ensuring that all candidates for the prestigious Oxford Sporting Blue are worthy of such an honour, and that all sports continue to follow the Oxford sporting ideal. He was a busy man and, but for his laid-back attitude to life, he would have been a harrassed one. Bruce took things casually, and inevitably the Boat Club had to run itself. As President McDonald would be responsible for sorting out the mess that Philp left behind, so he took a year's sabbatical from his undergraduate degree. This gave him time to concentrate completely on his own training and the restoration of order to the Boat Club. Thus relieved of the normal pressures of study, he had time to reassess the organisation of his crews and coaches, and determined to be a winning President. Initially, he more than anyone was prepared to listen to the criticisms that Clark came out with. Clark and McDonald had one thing in common – they had both lost the Boat Race, and neither wanted to do so again. Respectful of Clark's experience and that of the other Americans who would form his winning Boat Race crew, McDonald was prepared to listen and try to instigate changes. By all accounts, he was as unhappy about the way Topolski expected them to train as anybody was, and he let the Americans lead him in requesting changes, respecting their experience as the others did. 'He didn't try to lead us because he knew his experience and ability didn't warrant us following him,' Penney remembers. 'He seemed to want us to tell him what to change,' and after receiving their first training programme, they were thankful for his openness to their ideas.

The first week's training programme, dated 13 October 1986, included a total of nine outings on the water. The morning outings were scheduled for one-and-a-half hours on the water, whilst afternoon rowing was scheduled from 1.30 – 5pm. On top of the rowing they were scheduled to complete three sessions in the gym, each two hours long, with track-running to finish, one timed run and a sixteen-minute workout on the ergometer (with the score noted and given to McDonald 'for the record'), to be completed in the rower's 'spare time'. 'That's more training than we did for the World Championships!' Lyons exclaimed.

Three of the sessions would be supervised, two by John Pilgrim-Morris, and one by Steve Royle. This programme was just the beginning; it is customary to start the season slowly and build up the amount of time and the intensity of the training. They were all shocked by the content of their first programme: 'It was hard to envisage spending any more time than this training,' Fish explained. 'This programme already demanded that our weekend was taken up till at least 3.30pm both Saturday and Sunday, and three afternoons in the week were also completely taken up with rowing, and the programme doesn't even mention time taken to travel to and from training venues, which were not always in Oxford, let alone time for showering and changing. It was hard to imagine any time for studying, let alone experiencing any sort of normal student life at Oxford.' 'We couldn't believe that we were expected to follow the programme,' laughed Chris Penney, and Fish called McDonald to say so.

'He arranged a meeting between Topolski and ourselves at Brown's, the popular restaurant situated at the top of St. Giles, so that we could have a friendly chat and discuss how Topolski saw things going, and perhaps suggest a few changes that would make the training more efficient and less time-consuming.' By the time it came to the meeting, they had all tried Topolski's recommended training and had seen the rest of the guys try it, and they realised that the only reason anyone survived it was because they did the work at a very low intensity, or because they skipped some sessions. When there was a coach present, or when they trained alongside each other, being competitive athletes, the intensity of the workout increased. But most of the time the training was not efficient.

The Americans weren't prepared to carry on like that. They knew how to train, and knew what they were looking for in fast crews. 'It was quite an education to listen to them,' Royle told me. 'They used to stand before and after outings in long debates about the training they were doing, they knew a lot about the physiology of training and the benefits the various types of training had, and they used each other to sort out each aspect of the training programmes and the benefits and disadvantages.' But Topolski didn't witness these informative gatherings; had he been part of them from the start, they may have had a better understanding of each other's point of view. Instead, the meeting at Brown's was, as Huntington said, 'the start of something!'

Donald set the meeting up. He asked Gavin Stewart, Tom Cadoux-Hudson, Topolski and the five Americans, Lyons, Fish, Huntington, Clark and Penney, basically the core group of the 1986 squad. The idea was to sit down and discuss a way forward for that year so that they could ask McDonald and Topolski a few questions about the Boat Race and Topolski's training regimes. The American contingent had some very definite ideas about what they thought would make their training better. They wanted to include a day off a week, and they also wanted to change the gym training so that they concentrared on weight-lifting, just the lifts aimed particularly at strengthening rowing muscles, not every single possible lift or exercise Topolski could dream up. Finally they wanted to try to maximise the time training on the water, and to make the sessions shorter but more intense. Topolski was a bit perturbed by this, and interpreted their request for changes as requests to cut the work load. His interpretation couldn't have been further from the truth. Huntington remembers feeling that they had challenged him by making suggestions: 'He didn't seem open to discussion, but we hadn't gone there with the intention of challenging his authority, we'd gone to discuss the way forward.' But Topolski just wanted them to listen in awe to his story about His Boat Race. In his words, 'It's a funny old race, and it needs a special approach.' Topolski was trying to feel at home with his new squad, but he felt challenged and offended by their new ideas.

Gavin, a Boat Race romantic, was taught to row by Topolski, and probably understands the man's mentality better than most. He tried to explain his reaction: 'Topolski's method of coaching is different from most; he relies on creating a mission for you, a whole ethos for you to train around,' said Gavin, 'and that's what he tried to do for us in that meeting at Brown's.' He had a captive audience with the exception of Clark, who hated it when Topolski jumped off in to his verbal wanderings. He believes fervently that the only thing that makes the Boat Race different from any normal race is really to do with the power and tradition behind a race which is rowed under the eyes of thousands of Britons, many of whom have nothing to do with either Oxford or Cambridge. It's romantic vision which should never be spoiled for the world, but, as in any serious sporting event, for the competitors the race *must* remain in perspective. It is a practical problem, and whichever opponent applies the most forethought, carries the most skill and uses the best preparation will win. Topolski's preparation was different; he didn't see the race as a practical problem, it was a mystical one. He believed, and wanted his men to believe that the race was different and unpredictable. Everybody in the room listened to Topolski, who was a great raconteur. Clark grew anxious: he didn't want to hear this, he'd gone there to get things changed, and at this rate they would never discuss the best approach to train to beat Cambridge; everyone was being side-tracked by Topolski's marvellous story.

Clark's behaviour was unjustifiable, as, unable to contain himself any longer, he shouted Topolski down. It was a glimpse of the frustrated athlete that Clark had been all summer, but his own outburst was misunderstood as a personality clash between Clark and Topolski. Clark was trying to get some sort of urgency going, he wanted things changed, and he knew that the others didn't want to carry on like they had been over the last couple of weeks. They had agreed before they arrived that Topolski's training demands were too great and inefficient, yet here they were listening to him telling them that they were wrong, that the way they had trained to win their World Championship medals wasn't the way to win the Boat Race. Clark was agitated because he had believed Topolski last year and had seen that it wasn't true; they had a good crew this year, and if they trained effectively he knew that they could beat Cambridge by miles: rowing and racing, no matter what the event, is basically the same: it requires the expertise, and they had plenty of that. Clark wanted to make them greater. Topolski wanted to win too, he wanted another great crew, he wanted the Americans to enjoy his Boat Race, and he interpreted their complaints as teething problems of settling in to Oxford life. He listened to them but didn't hear what they were saying; there was no communication between them.

4

It is impossible to understand the 1987 dispute without a clear picture of Christoper Clark. Despite his not being the cause of the dispute, he was made a scapegoat for the actions of the Boat Race squad, and was painted in a very ugly manner by Topolski and McDonald and subsequently the British Press. Clark jokingly said to me whilst I was writing this, 'Don't destroy the image of me as a "black leather jacket, cruel, nasty, arrogant" character too much. It comes in handy at times when people try to give me a hard time!' Had he had the foresight to see the picture that was to be painted of him, he would have been wiser to have taken on the post of President when Topolski offered it to him in the summer of 1986. As President, he would have avoided the whole dispute because McDonald would have been just another oarsman; the powers of selection and control that go with the Presidency would have been Clark's, and it is likely that McDonald would not have been considered for the crew. As President, it is inconceivable that no matter what he did, that he would have been portrayed by the Press as a brattish, trauma-prone John McEnroe-type figure of the rowing world. More likely, the title of President would have shielded him from the harsh words of the Press, and his strong silences and pensive moods would have been interpreted as a will of steel, the characteristic of a forthright leader. He might even have been remembered as the American here who saved Oxford from another defeat! But Clark wasn't the sort of person to get excited by power and leadership, and such was his opinion of himself that he didn't consider himself Presidential material. He declined Topolski's request for him to be President, and remained 'just an oarsman', unconcerned with the honour bestowed upon those who preside. As 'just an oarsman', and one particularly good at defending himself, he attracted the sort of venomous attention normally associated with graffiti-scribbling adolescents. When you meet him and hear of him from the people that knew and worked with him, it's hard to imagine why. Far from being outrageous and uncontrollably obnoxious, he seems an amusing person, uncomfortable in the limelight.

Prior to his arrival at Oxford in 1986, Clark had enjoyed six years of rowing, and had followed a fairly standard development. Like many people, he started at college, rowing in his first freshman's Eight in 1977 whilst studying at the Orange Coast College. From there he went on to Stanford to study International Relations. During that year, Clark didn't row; he realised how much time rowing demanded, and was not prepared to compromise his study for rowing, at which he was not yet particularly good. A year away from the sport was enough: he missed it, and couldn't wait to get back in to a good crew. On arrival at Berkeley in 1980, with the prospect of being able to get into a good Eight, he rejoined the sport. He had the potential to be very good: his physique was right, his attitude to training was hard and enthusiastic, and his technical skill was developing quickly. He was inspired by winning, and thoughts of winning more and greater races spurred him on. After graduating in 1982, he joined three other CAL oarsmen to row and train in a Coxless Four, hopeful of selection for the US National Team. The Four improved tremendously over the summer, and they lost the National Trials by just one second to a Four in which his future partner and friend, Dan Lyons, was rowing.

Having rowed in a successful crew for a year, Clark was beginning to be noticed as a potential member of the US National Team. He is a naturally athletic person who had taken quickly to rowing, and whether he made it to the top would depend upon his commitment, direction from an experienced coach and good timing; with any squad system there is a certain amount of being in the right place at the right time. Being able and prepared to travel to train with the best members of the National Team helps, and there is a lot to be gained from training with the best. Selection for the American National teams differs slightly from the British National team selection; in Britain, selection trials are carried out throughout the winter and early summer.

Individuals and pairs are trialled over long and short distances and combinations sorted and swapped and re-raced, so that the crews that are put together supposedly contain the fastest individuals in the country. A definite ranking order for each oarsman and woman who put themselves up for team selection gradually develops over the winter as crews race and train regularly together, and this relies on the majority of rowers being collected at the same location for training.

In America, the sheer size of the country makes this selection procedure difficult to support, although in recent years they have tried to gradually introduce this type of selection. Basically there are two ways to be selected to row for America: the first is to be invited to one of the training camps put together specifically for selecting their 'priority crews'; the second is to go to a trials race in a crew of your own to race off for the 'non-priority' boats, the fastest crew to win a series of races being selected to go to the World Championships. Emphasis is placed upon the performance of athletes at the invitation-only training camps, maybe five or six during the summer months. The boats chosen as 'priority' boats differ each year, but usually include the Eight; these crews are supposed to contain the best oarsmen in the country. Having not made a 'priority' crew, oarsmen are free to form their own crews to race in the trials races for the 'non-priority' crews. This secondary system means that oarsmen who do get dropped, or maybe even don't get as far as the selection for the camp, can then go on and form their own crew and race off at the specified trials race, attempting to become a World Championship crew. It also allows oarsmen who don't want to get involved in the training camp selection system, or individuals who may have been ill or injured during the trials but think they are good enough to represent the country, to have a chance at selection. It is beneficial because oarsmen who may have been missed get a chance to prove themselves. The American Silver medal-winning Coxless Four, coached by

Ted Nash from Penn AC, is a prime example of such a crew. Two of the guys in that crew weren't selected to make the training camp for the Eight selection, but later went on to win the Coxless Four trials and a Silver medal at the LA Olympics.

In 1983 and '84, as a fairly unrecognised oarsman, Clark mistakenly opted to stay with the system he knew, and trained with others from his college at Berkeley in '83 in a Four, and then in '84 in a Coxed Pair with George Livingstone. Clark remembered the year well, and laughed nervously when he said they were crazy to try to get selected in the Coxed Pair. It was a comment typical of this introspective man. The Coxed Pair is primarily a strength event, usually reserved for the older, stronger and more experienced rowers. Given his time over again, he would have made an effort to try to get in with the squad earlier on; it would have involved more travelling and more effort, but he thinks it a better way to get selected rather than trying to train and learn under one's own steam and to get selected at trials races. But at the time they believed in each other and their ability to make it to the top, so they took what they saw as the clearest road of demonstrating their individual worth. In 1983 they were beaten by a second, and in 1984 the story was similar: Livingstone and he narrowly missed winning the Pairs trials race; however, they did get selected to compete at the Pan American Games, where they won a silver medal. Clark was beginning to make a name for himself in the US rowing world, having narrowly missed winning the 'non-priority' boat selection in both '83 and '84. In '85 he was invited to trial at training camp for the Eight. He had changed partners and boat, and was training in the Coxless Pair with Kirt Bausbeck, another Berkeley oarsman. This year he set his sights on selection for the golden boat, the Olympic Eight. Clark verged on making the final eight, but in the end Chief Coach Korzenowski dropped him for another oarsman, John Strodbeck, because Clark didn't 'swing well within the crew'. Clark had beaten Strodbeck not only on the ergometer, but also in the seat race trials. This was Clark's first experience of the subjective quirks of rowing selection; Strodbeck had been training under Korzenowski that year, and he hadn't. Huntington and two of the other rowers already selected for the Eight questioned Korzenowski 's decision to put Strodbeck in the crew instead of Clark, but Korzenowski stood his ground. The Eight finished third at the World Championships, narrowly missing the Gold by just .98 of a second. If Clark was that bit better than Strodbeck, and he believes he was, he may have made the difference between a Gold and a Bronze medal. However, this is a question that will remain unresolved for ever.

There is nothing unusual in disagreements over crew selection. The numerous factors that make a boat go fast, particularly a crew boat like the Eight, mean that frequently selection of individuals of very comparable ability is left to the coach's subjective opinion. The coach will make a selection decision based upon who seems to make the boat faster, rather than who demonstrably makes it faster. This is not just a quirk of the sport, but stems from one of the dilemmas in rowing: how do you quantify rowing ability? The methods used by the majority of coaches are as follows: performance on the ergometer, a dry land rowing machine which is designed to give a feel as close to pulling a blade through the water. In reality, the handle is attached to a chain which spins a flywheel. The harder the rower pulls the handle, the faster the wheel spins. The revolutions are measured to give a score equivalent to how far the 'boat' is travelling. The ergometer tests strength, co-ordination and endurance, and from the scores the truth about your power output and how much it changes during the duration of a timed piece of work can be recorded for everyone to see, yourself included. It represents the individual, personal aspect of rowing, testing the depth of your will, your drive, your tenacity and your raw strength without the impetus of team spirit or the competitive incentive of beating another boat. It doesn't, however, test the technical ability of an oarsman. Rowing is more than a power sport. It requires very precise co-ordination and balance to place just the spoon of the blade into the water and at the same time to apply maximum power to the blade to drive the boat forwards. The unpredictable movements of the water and the boat, and the movement of up to seven other oarsmen trying to achieve the same end, make the movement a skilful one, which requires more than just power. In the crew boat, the synchronism is as important as the strength of the individuals. The only way to test this ability is to run a series of 'seat races'. In this, two crews, usually four-oared boats, will race side by side over a set distance. At the end of the race, one oarsman will swap places with his opposite number in the other crew, and the new combinations are again raced over the same distance; by a comparison of the results the two individuals can be directly compared. The outcome of this type of trial can be dependent upon various factors: the boat type should be the same, as some boats are lighter or are heavier to row, and some are arguably a faster shape than others; the oarsmen should all be fit and healthy and prepared to give maximum output, and the stroke cadence must be the same for each crew. All being equal, seat racing can be a very productive method of trial, but it must be well-planned and is often most usefully used to prove to the oarsmen a result which the coach already suspects.

Despite not making the US Eight in 1985, Clark had had his best year of rowing yet; he was on the way up the rowing ladder. He felt fitter and more confident of his ability than he ever had, and was selected as one of the two 'spare' rowers to go with the team to the World Championships. His job would be to substitute for any of the rowers, in any crew, who became sick or injured during training or racing. It can be hard for the spare rowers to stay fit and motivated for the weeks after selection leading to the championships, especially as for many their goal would have been to be in the team themselves. To combat this, Clark, ever enthusiastic, spent his summer rowing in the 'Dirty Dozen' Eight which won the National Championships. At the championships, things turned for the better. During training, the strokeman in the Pair was injured, and Clark was asked to sub for him. Dan Lyons was the other half of the pair, and his assessment of the new combination was that it was the best Pair he'd ever rowed in. They proved their ability in the Petit Final by gaining a lead of ten seconds by the 1000m mark, eventually winning by over three lengths of clear water. The only regret about the whole occasion was that Lyons's partner had not accepted his injury sooner and allowed Clark to compete in the heats and semi-finals, thus giving them the chance to qualify for the final for the first to sixth places instead of the Petit Final, which races for the sixth to twelve places. By comparison of straight times between the two finals, Lyons and Clark would have finished third overall.

It is unusual for a substitute to race in the Pairs race, primarily because it is a difficult event, and more than any other crew relies on two men adapting to each other's skills to such an extent that their technique is identical: this can take months. For Clark and Lyons, the bond was immediate. There were obvious improvements that time and good coaching would put right, but for a scratch combination they were noticeably quick. Being so demonstrably successful was the break Clark needed, as coaches notice sparks of brilliance: Tor Nielson, the Italian team's 'emperor' of rowing was dumbfounded that Clark's ability had been allowed to slip through the system. 'Why hadn't he been rowing in the Coxless Pair, anyway?' he had asked. Korzenowski too was impressed, and suggested that Lyons and Clark continue in the Coxless Pair for the 1986 season. Even without his blessing, it would have taken a strong character to stop them; they were convinced that the Pair was their road to rowing success. 1986 was the year that Clark arrived at Oxford, filled with thoughts of next year's World Championships, and in the peak of condition. He would obviously need to train hard whilst in England so that he was fit and ready to jump into the Pair in the summer. He looked upon the Boat Race as an attractive way to stay fit and competitive throughout the long winter months, as had the other internationals who had graced Oxford waters over the years.

For the oarsman, the winter months represent cold weather, long sessions to improve stamina and technique, and a distinct lack of the exciting side-by-side sprint racing which oarsmen love. However, the long hard winter training is a necessary part of preparation for the summer racing season, and it is the time when technical faults can be ironed out and the necessary aerobic fitness and strength gained. Training for the Boat Race overcomes the boredom many associate with the winter months: it is a winter side-by-side race and because it is longer than the summer 2000m racing, the intensity of the long distance training over the winter is crucial. It is the ideal bait to keep oarsmen hungry for competition through the winter. Clark was looking forward to Oxford University, a diploma course to keep his grey matter intact, and a chance to race in the esteemed Oxford and Cambridge Boat Race. His hopes for an active exciting time were never dashed; academically and socially, the University more than fulfilled his requirements, although where rowing was concerned he quickly felt less sure that Oxford was a good idea. He arrived in a bad year, and instead of training amongst a squad of enthusiastic, fit, skilled oarsmen, he found that the quality of the rowers was not as good as he hoped. His answer was to carry on training in the same vein as he had done over the last three years of his rowing career; he jumped into a Pair with his old partner George Livingstone, who was also studying at Oxford at the time, and they worked out a schedule similar to the one they always used and trained together.

Of course they took part in the crew selection tests, the ergometers, the seat racing, and they enthused about the typical prankster nature of the guys from the OUBC. 'We got stuck into Oxford life and intended to make the most of it,' Clark remembers. 'For the most part we just tried not to get involved with Topolski in rowing terms, because we didn't have much time for his ideas. To be quite honest, I thought all that mystical Tideway bull ... he gave was just a ploy for the Press. If you knew anything about rowing, you couldn't really believe in it.' The only problem was that, by wanting to row in the Boat Race, they were obliged to spend a lot of time training under Toplski's regimes, and Clark wasn't ready for how important the Boat Race became to him, leaving him a personal dilemma about the training and Oxford rowing. He desperately wanted to row, but that meant being coached by people he had no respect for (in rowing terms), and following a programme which he did not believe was the best way to train. Clark talks convincingly about his first year at Oxford, and it was obvious both from him and Topolski that, where rowing was concerned, there was a professional respect between the two of them.

Off the water, they enjoyed each other's company. Topolski never missed a good party or a good prank: 'He was the perfect partner in crime when it came to having a good time,' Chris smirked. 'He was great company, and he certainly knew how to enjoy himself!'. In the games they played, they were well-matched, but as far as rowing went, they were miles apart.

The Boat Race was a race to be won, and when Oxford lost, Clark suffered terribly. Losing any great race is hard, but if you can see a constructive way to win it the next time you try, then the losing becomes easier to bear. You can divert your anger from losing into a plan for revenge, and that is exactly what Clark did next. The problem was that his plan involved a lot of changes, and one of them meant changing the infrastructure of the Oxford University Boat Club. He wasn't sure how, but he was determined to win, more determined than he would care to admit to himself or anyone else. He, like many Oxonians who had rowed and lost the Boat Race, was fuelled with a need to win the race.

Once the race was over, Clark was anxious to get back to the States, leaving behind him the problems of an antiquated boat club and his memories of the lost Boat Race. Topolski wanted him to stay around longer to follow the Boat Club on the many invitation trips to race abroad which they receive. Clark wasn't interested, and Topolski was furious that he could thrust aside the Boat Club and disappear without any apparent regard for whether he was needed to race in the Oxford Eight. Despite the fact that Clark had warned Topolski that he wasn't likely to be around to race in the summer, Topolski shot himself in the foot by promising the organisers of one particular race, against Clark's old University, Berkeley, that Clark would be racing. The race organisers had based some of their publicity around having the Berkeley veteran in the race. Clark not rowing was an embarassment to them and to Topolski. Clark hadn't committed himself to rowing for Oxford, but Topolski had hoping that the personal publicity would entice him to reconsider racing, but Topolski had based his hope on his own mentality, rather than on Clark's. Clark wasn't interested in public recognition; he rowed because he thrived on the sport, and at that time thoughts of the World Championships and his pair with Lyons filled his horizon. Unfortunately, his plans for that summer were destroyed when he badly strained the intercostal muscles on the left side of his ribcage during training. A nagging, painful injury, which has become increasingly common in oarsmen as rowing techniques change over the years, it results in a sharp pain through the ribs and round into the spine every time the oarsman places his blade into the water. The nature of the injury is such that if you change your technique slightly so that you don't hold your leg drive, you can lessen the pain and continue rowing. Compensation for injury usually results in another injury as you shift stress from one part of your body to another. Clark learnt this lesson when he strained the intercostal muscles on the other side of his chest. Injury at this late stage almost certainly meant that he wouldn't make the Championships. Champions placed in this dilemma will seek medical help, but as a rule find it very difficult to accept the advice that rest is the only cure. To the athlete who spends every day of his life pushing through the mental and physical pain generated by tired, sore muscles, accepting an injury, accepting pain which tells you to stop, can feel like defeat.

The result for Clark was dashed hopes for the World Championships. He had suffered two major blows in the space of four months, and everything he had worked for had come to an end. Lyons was able to join a Coxless Four for the World Championships, and came home with a gold medal. At least the injury hadn't destroyed his summer, and Clark was thankful for that. He returned to Oxford, very unfit after a lazy summer nursing his wounds; an ace at covering up his disappointments, and fuelled by two years of disappointment, he dived into the start of a new term and a new Boat Race year in his normal casual, but creative manner. The last year over and a new set of talent promised, he had everything to look forward to. He had four fellow American Internationals with whom to share the Oxford experience and to combat Cambridge. His injury had cleared up and, filled with friends from last year, Oxford felt like home. It wasn't until he returned to Oxford and received his first training programme from

Topolski that his disillusionment with Oxford rowing returned. He knew that with the help of the others things could change: after all, it was supposed to be a University Boat Club, a student boat which students run. First, he had to convince them that change was needed and that Oxford rowing could be better, much better, than it was.

5

A new term or a new year of student life life brings with it many demands; there are seemingly endless rounds of new tutors to meet and new timetables to be worked out, accommodation to be fixed, new friends to make and old acquaintances to be re-established. For the Boat Race oarsmen, there is also the start of a new season's training.

Much of the early weeks leading up to term and into November was spent training in Pairs, Sculling boats and Fours, much of it unsupervised. During these early weeks, everybody tries hard to let the rowing training take care of itself, the organisation and direction remaining the sole responsibility of the President and chief coach, who point newcomers in the right direction and lay out the plans for the coming year.

Training in small boats, largely under their own steam, the Americans were quick to establish their own routines in their training times; a set structure was something, as far as they could see, that Oxford didn't have. Individuals seemed happy to just carry out the training programme under the supervision of whichever coach was available, alone if no one was there. The Americans were shocked by the lack of structure, and offered suggestions for change, as well as registering their complaints about the amount of work on Topolski's training programmes. McDonald noted their queries and acted with diplomacy, promising action or talk with the coaching team where necessary. They weren't unhappy with the rowing, they hadn't had time to sort out what did and didn't happen at Oxford, they were surprised by the way things were run and by the heavy training schedules, and they were particularly surprised by the unrest among the other oarsmen. The early training schedules differed from the ones they had been used to at their colleges, largely because of the amount of time they were expected to spend training and racing in sculling boats, and the large number of extra activities which Topolski seemed to demand: timed gym circuits with an emphasis on speed, not quality, and timed runs; they were used to running, but not as a selection criterion. But it was the time spent sculling that they found the most bizarre. Since Topolski took over as Oxford's chief coach, sculling Head races, run throughout the winter months, have become a regular feature on the Oxford winter training programmes. Topolski, a master in a sculling boat himself, is a great believer that there are many advantages in learning to scull. He insisted that all his oarsmen should learn to scull, and used the results from the sculling Heads as a part of his final Boat Race crew selection. He believed that if a person could make a scull go fast, he was likely to be worth his salt in a crew boat.

A successful sculler demonstrates his individual ability to move a boat, and when transferred to a crew, this ability obviously makes him a worthy member. Poor performance at the sculling Heads was one particular gripe Topolski held against Clark in the dispute: McDonald was one of Oxford's best scullers, Clark one of the worst.

Some of the fastest rowing crews have been produced by putting the eight fastest scullers into an eight-oared boat; the famous Tideway Scullers School, a rowing club based alongside Chiswick Bridge on the Thames, concentrates on sculling training and forms many fast crews from putting the fastest scullers in to crew rowing boats. The principle of teaching individuals to scull before they learn to row is a good one, because the dexterity and balance required of a sculler is greater than that of an oarsman. However, there are many great rowers who cannot scull well. Andy Holmes is a fine example. Redgrave and Holmes were the fastest Pair in the world for three consecutive years; Redgrave is one of the fastest scullers in Britain, but Holmes goes no faster than a novice! Redgrave's other partner, Simon Berrisford, can scull, but not fast enough to finish even in the top ten in a British sculling Head, yet he too is one of the best rowers in the world. Nobody questions their rowing ability, despite their lack of skill in the single scull. For the Americans at Oxford, the story was similar: Lyons, Penney, Clark and Huntington, all successful international oarsmen, had reached the top rowing without ever really learning to scull. They considered the idea of learning to scull a novelty, but felt that their time spent flailing around in sculls to be rather wasteful. For most people, learning to scull well enough to get a good training effect from the time spent on the water takes the best part of a year. One usually spends the first few months in a sculling boat idling up and down the river mastering the balance, content with just staying upright. Learning to scull can be a cold and soggy pastime! Although fun, the Americans felt that learning to scull was not a particularly constructive way for themselves, or for the other OUBC members who couldn't really scull well, to spend their time. Rowing was their discipline, and they clearly felt that their time would be better spent training in Pairs, improving their technique.

(That year, the Oxford Women's Boat Club took on a new coach, Steve Gunn. Gunn had mainly coached schoolboys at Hampton School. Within the school system, the junior boys are taught to scull before they row. They usually found that, having spent a couple of years sculling in singles and crew sculling boats, the boys would then pick up rowing with greater ease and with more success. Experience in a sculling boat means that they quickly learn to be more sympathetic to the movements of the boat, and are more able to discern what makes a boat go fast, whilst also learning some important skills in boat/water management. Appalled by the standard of women's rowing at Oxford, Steve felt that teaching the girls to scull, as with the junior boys at his school, would be the best method for teaching some fundamental rowing skills. The idea was sound in theory, but in practice didn't work, because there simply was not enough time to teach the girls to scull well enough to benefit their rowing. The time that the Oxford girls spent on the water flailing about in sculls was time

Cambridge spent gaining more fitness and maximising their rowing technique. Cambridge won the Women's Boat Race easily! However, as a long term approach, it can be regarded as successful, as the girls from the Oxford crew that stuck with rowing and developed their sculling skills were the ones who made the better oarswomen.)

It seemed particularly odd to the Americans that they should be encourged to use their valuable hours of training drifting around the Isis gaining little fitness when Topolski was so keen on masses and masses of hard training; his favourite story is that the Americans just had no idea of the extraordinary physical demands that the Boat Race puts upon an oarsman. Supreme fitness, not a moment wasted, was his answer. However, sculling didn't seem to support this ethic. They saw the benefits of learning to scull very early on in training, before November, and after the Boat Race for the summer months, but saw the short term gain during the months of November through to the Boat Race in March as negligible for the majority of the poor scullers in the squad. Certainly, from a selection point of view, they could see no relevance in comparing the likes of McDonald and Pelham, who had been sculling for a couple of years now, and, say, Penney, or Huntington, or Clark, who showed no form at the sculling Head races because they had never really spent time sculling before. Topolski and McDonald obviously disagreed, and all of the athletes, experienced or not, had their performance at the sculling Heads duly noted as they struggled their way down the river reaches of Wallingford, Reading, Henley and Marlow. Indeed, in these races part of the fun seemed to be seeing who could stay afloat for the longest! It was certainly fun to have a laugh at World medallists navigating themselves in to the bank and getting tangled with the reeds as they tried to negotiate the bendy Head Race courses. The Americans had thought it impractical to scull from the start, but their enthusiasm never waned, although it clearly was not the sort of intense training they had expected from Boat Race rowing, and as term progressed and the novelty wore off, there was a feeling that things needed to change. They were anxious to get on with the whole of their Oxford lives, and they knew it was possible to train hard and play hard. Topolski's persistence in making them spend valuable training time learning to scull seemed to make a mockery of his pressure to maintain the intensity and fervent competitiveness in preparing for the race which he describes as 'the most brutal, harsh and uncompromising struggle of all sport'; it was 'annoying, to say the least', according to Fish.

Topolski's crew selection criteria were straightforward. He recorded ergometer test scores, sculling Head results, times to complete a weights circuit in the gym, weights lifted, timed runs and seat racing results. From these he selected his crew. The emphasis was on competition between the individuals in all the training, and was aimed at making the training sessions more intense, but intensity on the water didn't seem a priority. Out of the six test categories, four were indoor pursuits, not work on the water, not rowing. Everybody was aware of the scoring system and would work intensely in the gym and on the runs and, with one ergo session per week, three gym sessions and two timed runs, the work on the water suffered because the water workouts didn't seem like a priority. Rowing was always hampered, too. There were long drives to the different training venues, often too many people for the number of boats (or not enough), boats poorly rigged or equipment damaged or mislaid. These niggles were not exactly conducive to hard, intense, enjoyable outings, particularly as there was the thought of a gym session to return to. However, such observations were not new; for years, internationals who had trained at Oxford and rowed in the Boat Race had complained of the inconsistency of the training and the bad scheduling of the sessions. Steve Royle, who has been part of the Oxford team since 1977, indeed confirmed that these complaints were not new. In 1982/83, when Richard Yonge and Boris Rankov were Presidents, they had both individually voiced worries about Topolski's lack of continuity, and had wanted all sorts of changes to his training. There had been numerous internationals who had trained alongside the Boat Race squad but had basically done their own thing, worried that the training the whole squad were doing was not quite right.

Topolski never saw any justification for the complaints, because when he arrived to coach at the weekend or during the gym sessions, everybody was keen to perform in his presence; after all, he was doing the selection and was the man to impress. Unlike the majority of the British oarsmen, the Americans thought that when Topolski appeared they should voice their opinions about how the training was going and what could be improved. Their intentions were purely in the interests of speed. Had they known Topolski better, they would have avoided questioning him as they later learned past crews and internationals had done. On the odd occasions that they saw Topolski, their many questions and queries had been discussed endlessly amongst themselves. Having discussed things endlessly with McDonald too, they expected Topolski to at least be aware of how things were going, but he was only aware of what he saw with his own eyes. McDonald had obviously been selective in what he told Topolski. When he appeared to coach, Topolski expected his oarsmen to be enthusiastic to get on and be prepared for a very hard session. Their questions were either ignored or skimmed over which really annoyed them, as these were intelligent men and they didn't respect being treated as if they didn't know what they were talking about. 'Topolski didn't want anything to change,' said Huntington, 'because he couldn't see the need for change, he wasn't around to see all the training, and he was missing the really bad bits.' Topolski too was annoyed: he didn't like what they were saying, he didn't like having his authority challenged, and why should he? He had coached many Boat Races before, and this year he was determined was to be no different; he interpreted what they were saying as a cop-out, a refusal to train as hard as he wanted them to. They did want to spend less time training, but they wanted to increase the intensity of the training, increase the quality and make the training more efficient.

Topolski's interpretation of the situation wasn't helped by Clark, who was having a lot of trouble getting back into training. His ribs were cured, but he had started the season very unfit. That didn't stop him making suggestions about changes to the training programmes; he was part of the squad and felt no qualms about being involved in decision-making about training, but Topolski thought he should be knuckling down and just training, not making suggestions at all. Of course, Clark's unfitness didn't in any way cloud his decision-making capabilities, but to Topolski only present form speaks; that is part of his ethos: 'train hard to show me how fit you are, and I will recognise you.'

To add to Clark's problems, he had volunteered to be the one oarsman who would change sides and learn to row on bowside, to correct the imbalance of having nearly all the best oarsmen on strokeside. Topolski had asked for a volunteer who would be prepared to change. Clark fancied the challenge, and so offered. In retrospect, after a month of trying and getting nowhere, it would have been better for him to swap back, not only because he was finding it almost impossible to settle rowing on bowside, but he also seemed to be plagued with endless bouts of colds, coughs and the flu. Changing sides and an unhealthy amount of illness did nothing for his confidence or his rowing. His attitude and his frustrations were inevitably vented upon the system which he wanted to change. One way and another, he was able to blame his bad luck upon the training programmes they were expected to follow, but being constantly overtired and unhappy with his rowing did nothing to help the situation. Had there been more continuity in the coaching, a good coach would have picked this up. His friends did, but he needed someone with authority to direct him. As it was, he received no direction, and continued wasting a lot of energy and time. His sulky, aggressive attitude made everyone wary of him, and accounts for the lack of respect many of the British oarsmen had for him in the period before Christmas.

He later rectified these bad feelings towards him when he returned to England to the training camp after Christmas. At the camp he was finally allowed back on strokeside, and that, combined with the rest he had had over the Christmas vacation, set him back on to the road to fitness. During that time, he rowed with the provisional second crew because Topolski rightly thought that he needed time to re-establish himself. As he got fitter and back on form, far from being disruptive or sulky, he became an inspiration to the men he rowed with.

Before Christmas, whether fit or not, Clark believed he still had the right to speak out about the things that were wrong with the system, and his American friends, closer to him than most, respected his right to do so; just because he was having problems getting back on form did not automatically render his opinions worthless. They knew and respected him and his ability. Topolski was free to interpret the suggestions as grumbling, whining complaints to be pacified and then ignored. He obviously thought of them as a weak, complaining squad which needed to be bullied into doing some hard work, but he couldn't have been further from the truth; these men had the determination it takes to reach the top. They knew what it took, and they were prepared to try and discuss their thoughts to try to change things for the better from the oarsmen's point of view. Topolski's attitude muddled them to the extent that they couldn't really get to grips with what was going on. The whole squad talked constantly about simple changes which could be made to make life simpler. They talked to the other coaches, who listened and agreed that changes 'x, y and z' were a good idea, but when they tried to instigate the agreed changes, they were told that wasn't the way things were done. Topolski would often get mad or upset, and there would be an embarrassed silence, then everything would continue unchanged. 'It was as if he thought that we just wanted to feel as if we had some say in what went on, that if he listened to us and agreed with us, we wouldn't notice if nothing changed! He asked us to do things that were just not on, then when we told him it wasn't possible he would leap into his spiel about the Boat Race being different from anything we ever rowed in before, as if it would help us rationalise going back on everything we'd talked about; if we'd known that Topolski wasn't prepared to change anything, we'd have been more armed to cope with the situation. As it was, we didn't, and it meant a lot of frustration for all of us, Topolski included,' Lyons explained. Their requests were rational and demonstrably sensible, but Topolski wouldn't listen, and they were unsure what it would take to make him listen. 'Topolski was out of touch with the oarsmen and their problems,' said Royle. 'They are intelligent men, logical in the way they thought, and they asked for changes that would have made life easier for all the rowers.'

As Christmas approached and nothing changed, they were reaching a deadlock. Topolski felt he had lost control of the squad, and the squad felt as if they had no control of their destiny. The Boat Race wasn't theirs anymore. In the weeks leading up to Christmas the arguments became more and more frequent and more confrontational. Topolski was convinced that they weren't training hard enough and that the oarsmen were all becoming too cocky. He had proof: they had raced the Fours Head of the River Race in early November and had not done as well as he expected them to. Traditionally the Fours Head is the first time that the two Universities get a chance to compare each other's squad performance, and gives everybody a taste of things to come. It is a winning move in the Boat Race game if you do well. With all the speed and power of the Americans, Topolski quite obviously expected his team to do well, but they didn't. Their first crew home, Hull, McDonald, Huntington and Cadoux-Hudson, finished eighteenth, four places behind the fastest Cambridge Four. The second crew, Leach, Lyons, Penney and Clark, was a further ten places down, sixteen seconds behind the first Cambridge Four. Topolski was outraged by the performance, and put it down completely to a lack of training. From then on, he was vehement that they were going to train harder than ever before. Topolski was the first one to despair. On Saturday, 29 November, after their outing at Radley, a four mile stretch of the Thames just outside Oxford, for the first time, Topolski was greeted by a complete refusal to complete a part of the training programme. They had all previously agreed that Saturdays would constitute just one long hard outing, except on days when they would be racing other crews. But, driven by his personal promise to make them work harder, he told them there would be another outing, to work on some technical faults, whilst the video of their rowing which he had just shown them was still clear in their minds, he said. The boys weren't impressed. They were tired of trying to fulfill Topolski's demands for more training, and despite Topolski's attempts to rationalise the situation, they refused to go out rowing again. The whole squad just upped and left Radley and Topolski without completing a second outing. Topolski's disregard for their agreements and their physical condition was unforgivable; they didn't feel good about the confrontation, but felt pushed to demonstrating that they couldn't go on like this. They had to show him that they didn't take kindly to being ignored. 'It was pointless going out,' said Penney. 'Everyone was very tired, we'd had a good outing and done some useful work. There would've been no point.'

The second outing was scheduled according to the programme, but this was because the programme was written before the agreed changes were instigated. Topolski had tried to use arguments about their bad performance at the Fours Head to demonstrate how they could not afford to do as he said, but the oarsmen considered his arguments as ridiculous: 'He was being irrational taking out our loss at the Fours Head by saying we lost because we didn't train hard enough,' said Gavin Stewart. 'But he didn't really have a leg to stand on, the whole race was a farce.' Topolski had split the best oarsmen amongst the different crews, so that instead of having a first, second and third crew he had several crews of approximately the same standard. It was a useful way to get everyone rowing together and made training more competitive, but this strategy was unlikely to win the Fours Head. Had he wanted to win, he should have put out the strongest possible combinations. The Fours Head is noticeably unpredictable, and this year was no exception: each crew had its own problems. In Huntington's Four, Hull was steering, but he'd never steered a Coxless Four before, and he'd never raced on the Tideway either. The obvious result was that he steered all over the place, not really taking advantage of the stream, and his violent manoeuvres with the foot rudder made it difficult for the crew to maintain any form of constant speed or balance. Taking the correct line in a race on the Tideway can gain you a lot of seconds over a crew which is wandering all over the river; it is a big river with a fast current, so to be in the centre of the fastest running part is crucial. The other Four were hampered by having to race in an old Aylings boat which was much too small for them and very heavy, and which got heavier as it took on water in the rough: not the ideal racing machine for a winning crew. They rowed the course taking in water every stroke of the race, and Fish remembers they had to get some help to lift the boat out of the water at the end as it was so heavy. When the crews finished the day, their combined problems made it a laughable event; they had been badly prepared for that paricular race and thought it best to accept their respective defeats objectively. However, Topolski didn't agree: he took the result as a poor show and blamed their bad attitude.

Topolski went home from Radley distraught. He couldn't seem to get these guys to do as he wanted. He told McDonald later on the phone that there was 'no point' in his coming back because he didn't believe in them anymore, and they 'don't believe in me'. He resigned. McDonald later rang Royle to ask him to be Chief Coach: he thought it might be better for all concerned if Topolski was asked to come back as finishing coach for the last two weeks before the race and was not involved in the day-to-day management over the next few months. Royle declined the offer because, he said, it would have been very bad politics for him to just step into Dan's shoes like that. He also said he thought it unlikely that Topolski would come back and act as finishing coach if he, Royle, had taken over his job. Royle didn't believe that Topolski really meant to resign, nor that the oarsmen really wanted to lose him; he based his judgement on his experience of the Boat Race over the last ten years. There had been previous occasions when international oarsmen or past Presidents had reacted badly to Topolski, and Royle acted to smooth everyone's egos so that they could get back on working terms with each other. 'I try to use gentle persuasion to try to steer the oarsmen in the direction that is best for the Boat Race,' said Royle, 'it is the students' race, but sometimes when tempers get frayed the rowers are capable of making the wrong decision. Losing Topolski like that was, I thought, wrong for the race.' Royle felt that standing back from the direct arguments was the best possible way to give them the best advice. Once pacified, McDonald did ask Topolski back. In deciding to do so, he made a change of mind to accept Topolski and to tolerate his quirks and lack of communicative skills as other Presidents had done before him. It is a shame that he did not discuss and explain his decision to the rest of the squad, but then, as Royle said, 'McDonald was not a good communicator. He never really brought the problems or his decisions out into the open. That was a major failing,' particularly, I think, because the rest of the squad were very much in touch with their own thoughts and feelings. This would have enabled them to have understood, as McDonald did after his talk with Steve Royle, that it was better for them to do their own thing and not to argue with Topolski. That certainly seems to have been how past Presidents had solved the dilemmas generated by Topolski's demands.

6

Losing Topolski would be reviewed dramatically by the British Press. After all, he was somewhat of an 'easy hero': not only had he coached the winning Boat Race crew twelve times, but he never tired of their attention and always had a juicy story for them when they wanted one. It would make great news that he had resigned because his oarsmen refused to abide by his training programmes. It would be awkward and embarrassing for McDonald, who, being President, would have to take the brunt of their questions. The situation had to be sorted out and, with Royle's refusal to take over where Topolski left off, McDonald called upon three old blues, Mike Mahony, Graham Jones and Boris Rankov, to advise him. He then called a meeting with the Americans and Gavin Stewart, who as Vice-President would go as representative of the rest of the Boat Club. At this meeting it was pointed out how differently the individuals interpreted the current situation, and how divided they stood in their ideas for how they should progress. As the supposed leader of this gathering, McDonald was short on authority; he wasn't in the same league as the rest of them in rowing terms, and he hadn't had as much experience of the running of student boat clubs as the rest of them. He didn't really have enough expert knowledge to comment on whether the suggestions the Americans were making were valuable. His authority came only from his nominated title of President and, aware of that, he pretty much let them lead the discussions to decide upon an appropriate settlement which he could authorise and would get the Boat Club a chief coach again.

Clark and Fish suggested that it was time for a change.

Everybody in the squad was unhappy with the way things were going, and they suggested accepting Topolski's resignation and starting afresh. For Clark, there were a whole number of reasons why this would be a good idea, not least of all because he had no respect for Topolski's ability as a technical coach. Fish, too, doubted Topolski's technical know-how. 'He has the concept behind the look all sorted,' he explained. 'But I really doubted that he knew what the "right" look was.' They were also convinced that Topolski would never accept any of the changes they had suggested; he had demonstrated that, no matter how hard they tried to talk to him, he wasn't prepared to listen. Clark agreed that he had a hatred of criticism and perceived that they had severely challenged his ego, and therefore concluded that it would be better if he resigned. Fish was acutely aware that, as professionals, they couldn't work with him because Topolski wasn't prepared to pander to the needs of the oarsmen, or to give them the help that they needed to perform. As a cox, he saw that a part of his job was to be aware of those needs and to monitor when the athletes were having a hard time. The oarsmen should be provided with the conditions to allow them to perform to the best of their ability. McDonald was prepared to discuss this option, although he had already spoken to Royle and was fairly convinced that they should ask Topolski back: in the back of his mind still lurked the thought that a new chief coach would not be a bad idea. Gavin remembers McDonald being quite open to the idea that perhaps Topolski wasn't the right person to coach this year's Boat Race crew, although Boris pointed out, as Royle had done, that he had been unsure of having Topolski in charge when he was President, but it had worked out well in the end.

It is often said that only in the United Kingdom do we have a particular love of the old and a seeming contempt for the new, but in this case it was primarily the American members of the meeting who cut short the suggestion to find a new coach. Lyons, Huntington, Penney and the Australian, Jones, took heed of Boris's words and decided that it wasn't a good idea to let Topolski resign. They were prepared to write off his resignation as typical of his character and as a reaction sparked off by their confrontation. They didn't really see the need for Topolski to go. In the back of their minds they held on to the belief that they could all come to an amicable arrangement. They still wanted to install a sense of proportion upon Topolski's training schedules and to come to some arrangement with regard to the ridiculous hours they were spending on the river and travelling to it, but they didn't see why Topolski should not agree to this. Lyons in particular didn't want to destroy the Oxford Boat Race by being a party to losing Oxford's most respected coach. Lyons is a great romantic at heart, and he was rather taken by the idealism Topolski represented. However, Topolski's obsession with the amount of training they were doing was still a key topic. Gavin, having been under Topolski's training for four years, assured everybody that his expectations this year were worse than ever before, and that despite being renowned for his ridiculous schedules, this year he had gone over the top. He, perhaps more than anyone, had a certain empathy with Topolski, and wanted to see him continue to coach the Boat Race. Gavin was thankful for Lyons's support, particularly as he respected and understood the coach's obsession and passionately felt that he was a part of the Boat Race tradition that the Americans had no right to interfere with. This, though, was probably the last time that Lyons would feel any sympathy for Topolski; at this point he was fired up by what they later referred to as Topolski's 'Wizard of Oz' disguise.

Lyons loved the romantic traditions that Oxford exudes, having been a part of a similar sort of set-up in the Naval Academy where tradition remains an important way of life for the recruits. He thought that he intuitively knew the desires which would be driving Topolski. He dearly wanted to give Topolski and Oxford the fastest Boat Race crew ever, but he was aware that, to do so, Topolski would have to curb his driving force until nearer to the race, when his passion could be usefully exploited. In his heart, he was not happy with suggestions to let Topolski resign. He thought it would be too sad to allow Topolski to go without this one great victory. In the months that followed, this sentiment for him would change, and all his respect and understanding would turn to pity: for the moment, however, they all agreed that to curb Topolski's ambitious programme they should work out a set of conditions under which everybody, Topolski included, could work, the main priority being to lower the amount of time wasted travelling to and from training venues and the endless hours wasted on the water, which they felt could be changed if they were better prepared before they set off for each training session.

Having decided to form a sort of contract, the atmosphere remained charged whilst they worked out what they wanted. A regime of 'core time' was their formula for curbing Topolski's over-enthusiastic training programmes. 'Core time' laid out the number of hours they were prepared to spend training, and what they expected from the organisation of the club. The agreement gave McDonald more responsibility in checking that coaches and training sessions were organised and boats rigged and ready. McDonald left the meeting with a copy of an agreement laid out in the training programme with suggestions for the changes which the rowers would be prepared to abide by. Almost all of them were now happy that things would change for the better, as they reasoned that, by returning, Topolski would be agreeing to some of their earlier suggested changes, but this time it would be a firm written-down agreement.

Clark, however, left that meeting believing that nothing would change.

Fish had decided to bury his own ideas for Topolski's dismissal, and respect the opinions of his rowers. He was, and remains to this day, a staunch believer in the ownership of the Boat Race being the oarsmens, and the priority being that they should make their own decisions about how the Boat Club should be run. He left the meeting ready to ensure that the agreed actions were taken. This was going to be a hard job: Topolski had never before changed his ways for anyone. In the past, many Internationals had given up trying to get his blessing for changes in training. Instead, they had just ignored his programmes and carried on in their own way without his blessing, refusing to make an issue of it. Royle had effectively told McDonald that Topolski was worth having as a coach because of his tremendous skill in preparing a crew in the final build-up to the race. For the rest of the year, his quirks were better ignored; McDonald was prepared to do just that, but it is a shame he didn't communicate this to the Americans. This philosophy had not occurred to them, and they assumed that if it was accepted, the agreement about 'core time' would stand.

Not surprisingly, all parties were later to resent the decisions taken at that meeting, their retrospective thoughts being indicative of where blame would lie in future disputes. Lyons, Huntington and Penney later realised that Clark and Fish had been right. Topolski would never listen to their suggestions because, by the time they got to the stage of that first walkout, his feathers were too ruffled. Topolski did agree to come back and coach when McDonald asked him to and he once again agreed to abide by the suggestion made in the 'core time' document. But his agreement didn't stand for long as he was offended by the document and ultimately expected the rowers to relax their agreements. He simply didn't believe that they would expect to follow what had been laid down. He obviously thought they just needed to win the argument; it was as if they were talking different languages. It is common for international business deals to go wrong because of language or nationality differences. Americans, for example, tend to be much more literal in their interpretation of language than the British. A statement that nothing will be changed means literally that to an American. The smallest deviation on unimportant matters, even if the deviations themselves are agreed as being desirable, is taken as betrayal of the original contract. British people tend to be more pragmatic, and when they say nothing will change, they mean nothing of substance will change, but that individual adjustments may be necessary to meet changing circumstances. Topolski was clearly demonstrating his right to be pragmatic, and the Americans were being typical when they set the agreement in the meeting at Mansfield. They expected the conditions to be adhered to. They truly believed that the conditions they had written down were the best way forward, and they expected Topolski to come back to discuss the parts he didn't agree with. There may have been further discussions between Topolski and McDonald, but they were never informed of these and, thus, they expected Topolski to abide by the agreement in the same way that they would; any breaks in the agreement gave them justification to make an issue. Had Topolski expected to be allowed to make slight changes to the programme, then there may have been a case for accusing both sides of being typically nationalistic, but Topolski's expectations went further than that, and it wasn't long before he was trying to regularly stick extra outings and the same old gym routines back into the training programmes. That the relationship reached such a low point that the rowers felt they could only trust the coaches if everything expected of them was written down, is representative of the poor communication.

Topolski had been in control of the Boat Club for years and had never had his control disputed. Many will feel that this should have been the case this year too, and that the oarsmen should not have challenged his decisions, but it is after all the oarsmen's race, and they should have a right to question its running. Royle said he was trying to run it by remote control and the oarsmen could see it wasn't working; they didn't like that, and so they asked for changes. Topolski and McDonald later said that if they had told the whole squad that if any of them weren't prepared to abide by Topolski's demands they should leave the squad then and there and not row, the later dispute would never have happened. Why he should have the right to do this, I question; however, had they knuckled down to his demands it is doubtful whether they could have avoided the ensuing battle, because the issue of training became secondary when the process of selecting the crews began.

7

After Christmas, the Oxford squad headed to London for a two-week training camp on the Tideway; a little Christmas and New Year festivity goes a long way towards maintaining a healthy verve for life, but does little for fine tuning a rower's physique. Returning to a training camp two weeks before the start of term is the best way to rapidly refocus attention on racing, as well as to regain any fitness which may have been lost. The camp is usually the venue of the first really intensive trialling, and marks the beginning of crew formation for the rapidly approaching race. Inevitably, certain individuals who haven't made the grade will be dropped as the squad is cut down to more manageable proportions. By Christmas, the squad has been rowing together for nearly three months, and each individual has a comparatively clear idea of his chance of a seat in one of the two crews, either as a potential Isis or Blue Boat candidate. A grey area exists only for the last few places in each crew, and the process of crew selection begins in earnest.

This year, Topolski seemed particularly keen to get the crews selected as soon as possible. The most obvious reason for this was that there was a big difference between the potential Blue Boat and Isis boat candidates. The Blue Boat was pretty much going to select itself, with four American Internationals and Cadoux-Hudson: there were only three places left to select. After such a fractious winter, Topolski would have little to gain from delaying the crew formation; it would be better to settle the two crews and give them both time to develop their full potential. Early selection is something Topolski, as a rule, didn't abide by, normally preferring to keep all the oarsmen under threat of not making the Blue Boat should they for one moment be lax in their training. This fanatical competitive element was the basis upon which all Topolski's training was based. When he used to row, he had thrived upon fighting to make the last place in a crew, often driving himself into the ground to do so, and he felt close to those oarsmen who had the same determined, hardened attitude.

Topolski's sudden desire to sort out the crew order in the early days of January was uncharacteristic, but under the circumstances understandable. Having just got back his position as Chief Coach, no doubt he was anxious to settle the Americans together in the boat. They could then concentrate their energies upon being the fastest Oxford Eight ever to have rowed the Boat Race.

Early Seat Race trials at Thorpe Park prior to the Christmas break had clearly demonstrated a rank order amongst the rowers. The order was pretty much as expected: the Americans and Cadoux-Hudson led the field, closely followed by Stewart and Hull. Pelham and Ward came next, but there was little to choose between them. The races were in Fours over a distance of four-and-a-half minutes. A noticeable difference between crews would show by a win by about a half a boat length. Over the four days, Topolski raced all the strokeside and bowside contenders for a place in the Blue Boat. When they left Thorpe, the order, best man first, put Huntington for strokeside a clear leader, a length faster than Penney. Penney beat Stewart, but there was little to choose between those two; Stewart then beat McDonald by two-thirds of a length, and Gleeson was just half a length behind him. On bowside, Cadoux-Hudson came out on top, followed closely by Hull. Hull beat Pelham by three-quarters of a length, and Pelham beat Ward by half a length. Although there wasn't much in it, that meant that third and fourth on bowside respectively were Pelham and Ward. Leach and Baird were raced, but seemed considerably slower then the other four and would be unlikely to make the Blue Boat selection. Both Clark and Lyons had left Oxford, Lyons on 10 December and Clark the day before the squad went to Thorpe. Both were suffering badly from flu, and had wisely decided not to attend Thorpe but to go back to the States for a break.

There is no point in racing seat races when infected with a virus: it's comparable to cutting your own throat. If you lose a race because of illness it will undoubtedly be used as evidence against you if it comes to the crunch! They were better off taking the time to fully recover, so that they returned after Christmas virus-free and ready to go. The whole squad had been rife with colds, coughs and flu throughout November and December, and many of the members were not as fit as they might have been. For example, in the two-week period leading up to the Trials Race in December, there was not one day when both crews did not have somebody from the crew missing because of illness. The two weeks leading up to Christmas were similar: there was hardly a day when at least two of the squad weren't off sick. You have to expect a certain amount of illness within a squad training as hard as the Boat Race crews do throughout the winter, but this year seemed to be a particularly bad one for Oxford.

It was quite unsettling to have oarsmen constantly missing because of illness, particularly when certain members missed Seat Race trials. Every oarsman, particularly the ones on the verge of making a crew, is anxious to see opponents trialled, and it is disturbing if someone you thought you would get a chance to race misses the trials. Had Clark and Lyons been present at Thorpe, they would both have been trialled on bowside, thus changing the bowside ranking considerably, probably placing Clark in contention for the last bowside seat with Pelham and Ward. Clark was still finding rowing on bowside very difficult, and was anxious to change back to strokeside, but Topolski was determined not to let him. Pelham and Ward were obviously anxious to see Clark change back, as it would increase their respective chances of a place. They also knew that it made sense to have Clark in on strokeside where he had proven his ability over the years.

For the strokeside seats, Stewart had beaten McDonald, despite unfair circumstances: Stewart had been at all the trials, and had been in one of the racing crews for two days. McDonald, however, had taken two days off from the races to attend a family wedding, and thus came into the races fresh. McDonald's results, compared with Gleeson's, left little to choose between the two of them, considering that Gleeson had been racing all weekend and McDonald was fresh. They weren't actually raced against each other, but a process of elimination, comparing the results against people that they had both raced, allowed this conclusion.

With these results in mind, the squad left Oxford for a Christmas break, each of them weighing up their own personal chances of a place in the crew and thinking of who they would have to beat to get that place. Clark spoke to Fish and Huntington during the vacation, and they both told him that it looked as if McDonald's days as a contender for the crew were limited. They were assuming that Topolski would have to trial Clark on strokeside, where he performed his best. Clark had decided before he left England that he couldn't cope with rowing on bowside any more. The only problem was that Clark would oust McDonald from his seat.

As soon as the oarsmen arrived back after Christmas, Topolski leapt into the serious business of finalising the crew. His plan of action was to measure performance on the ergometer and to carry out more seat racing with the members of the squad who formed the grey area between the two crews. That meant Clark, McDonald, Pelham, Ward perhaps, and Gleeson. At selection times, tension rises and speculation is rife. Everybody is determined to demonstrate that they deserve consideration for a place in the crew. One thing that was certain was that McDonald was seen as a target whose place was up for grabs. Gleeson wanted a chance to race McDonald, and so did Clark. Ward and Pelham felt sure that Clark would beat McDonald on strokeside, and that equally he wouldn't beat them on bowside. The problem everybody saw was that McDonald wasn't going to give up his seat in the Blue Boat, particularly not to Clark. Winning the Boat Race meant everything to him. He had dedicated a year of his life to being President of the Boat Club despite tremendous financial pressures, and he'd invested an enormous amount of effort in training for the race. This was to be the race of his life, and as President his job was to 'select and manage all University crews'. It would be hard, really hard, for him to give up his seat, even to a better oarsman. Most of the Oxford squad had a sinking feeling that, even if it was proven that he wasn't the best man for the job, McDonald wasn't going to relinquish his seat. So predominant was the feeling that the President was trying to save his seat, that the 'McDonald fudge factor', aptly named by Justin Cheetle, one of the better Isis rowers, became quite a talking point, especially on days when Topolski announced 'trials' of any kind. It had been a talking point since after the Trials race in December, and was becoming increasingly more so as selection grew imminent.

As time went by, Topolski and McDonald had become closer and closer, to the extent that Mcdonald was probably the only person in the squad who Topolski was in close contact with. He was alert to the pressures on the President, as a chief coach should be, and no doubt he was well aware of the increasing animosity towards him. Topolski knew he would have to trial McDonald, but in sympathy for him, I don't think he wanted to. As far as he was concerned, McDonald was very fit, had trained hard and had been a good President. The more Topolski shielded him, the more he became a target. That the others should want to race him was natural; it was also natural that any signs of the coach protecting McDonald would be interpreted as favouritism and lead to increased animosity toward the President. The 'fudge factor' had become hot gossip at the trials at Thorpe; McDonald was absent until the last day of the trials, so that his turn for seat racing came only when his opposition were tired from the three previous days' racing. After Christmas too, McDonald was left out of the racing Fours when they carried out the seat races on the Tideway; instead, he rowed in a spare Four, which went off to work alone whilst the others endured more trials. His ergometer score, too, was fudged. Not the score itself, but, where everyone else was allowed just one recorded score, McDonald was given a second chance; his first score wasn't good enough to beat

Clark. His second one was. By the end of two weeks in London, the 'McDonald fudge factor' had become a very real problem.

It is interesting at this point to compare the differences in opinion the oarsmen held about who should be in the crew, and who Topolski had lined up for the eight places. The first three on each side were straightforward: on strokeside, Huntington, Penney and Stewart. The fourth person would be either Clark, McDonald, or maybe Gleeson. Topolski wasn't considering Gleeson, and wasn't prepared to try him; at Thorpe, Huntington suggested to Topolski that it would be a good race. Topolski said he hadn't thought about it, but maybe he would race him against McDonald. However, he didn't bother. Until after the Christmas vacation, Topolski also didn't consider Clark, because as far as he was concerned, Clark was rowing on bowside, despite the fact that he was doing so badly. Topolski had him slotted in on bowside, and Topolski and McDonald wanted him to stay there.

On bowside, presumably Lyons was top (although most expected Topolski to confirm his position by seat racing when he arrived back after Christmas). Cadoux-Hudson and Hull had performed convincingly for their places. For the final seat on each side, there would be a battle. Pelham and Ward had been fighting a private war all year. Pelham had a definite advantage in the sculling and in the strength weight tests, but on the concept ergometer tests and the speed circuits in the gym Ward had proven that, despite his inferior strength, he was fit and that he could apply his power. In the boat, Pelham had beaten Ward by one-and-a-quarter lengths in their first race at Thorpe, and then in a second race later on that weekend, when both oarsmen were tired, by only one quarter of a length. The fight wasn't over yet. Pelham, a curious character, known for his manic attitude to training and racing, can be a bit of a nightmare to row with, his technique a little less than perfect. He's a real crash and bash oarsman, admired mostly for his incredible strength, endurance and warrior-like attitude; one thing is certain, Hugh Pelham would never give in. The only real problem with Pelham was that, in a crew, because of his extra efforts and lack of technical skill, sometimes he just didn't fit in. It is not always the strongest, meanest racer who wins: in a crew the combined skill is just as important. Ward was favoured more for his skill in a crew boat, and most of the oarsmen thought he would take the last bowside seat rather than Pelham, but he still had to prove he was worthy of it..

McDonald was not the only person under pressure from the squad. As far as Clark was concerned, he himself was fairly unpopular by the time Christmas came. He hadn't been training as hard as the rest of the squad because of recurrent illness and his problems coming to terms with rowing on bowside, and so his training had been sporadic. He hadn't demonstrated the skill the English guys believed he had. Ward and Pelham were concerned that Clark was going to get the last seat on bowside, and they wanted the chance to beat him in a Seat Race. Ward believed that Clark should row on strokeside, or not at all. They discussed the way they felt with Topolski whilst they were away racing for Oxford in Seville over Christmas. The pleasantness of the sun and sea and the fun that these racing trips provide gave them the perfect opportunity to suss out Topolski's next moves, and to talk more openly about individual chances. The holiday atmosphere gave Pelham and Ward a chance to convey their individual wishes to race Chris Clark. They were well aware of Clark's inadequacy on bowside and his apparent lack of motivation for training over the last few weeks; his inability was their stairway to a Blue. 'Topolski knew we could beat him,' said Ward. 'He agreed with us and promised that he would have to prove his worth to get a seat. But he was quite protective about whether he thought we would get in. He knew that Clark was good, that was why he'd accepted Clark's suggestion that he should change sides originally, to even up the talent on both sides.' Pelham and Ward were worried that Clark would get a seat just because of his previous prowess. They wanted him to prove his ability, and knew he couldn't do it on bowside. Topolski's promise reassured them that they would get a fair chance.

Clark himself was suffering from a real confidence

problem rowing on bowside. 'I just couldn't do it,' he remembered, 'and it really bugged me. I was determined to get it sorted, but the harder I tried the worse I got, or so it seemed. It was terrible.' He left in December, looking forward to the peace and quiet of his home. It had to be said that not having him around was a relief to everybody else, too. There is nothing worse than pushing yourself to your own limits of training and being tormented by a dissatisfied member of the squad who can't complete the training because of his own problems. Selection time is a time for yourself. There is no compromise, and other people's inadequacies tend to cause the reaction: 'Ah well, if you can't take the pressure, you'd better get out'. Everything is analysed in terms of rowing: if you get injured, you're jacking out; if you sulk, you can't handle the pressure; if you lose control, you're trying to protect yourself. The intolerance of 'abnormal' behaviour is worse the further down the performance scale you look, because individuals fighting for the last places are looking hard for a seat in a crew.

Clark had proved nothing that year: as yet he hadn't been seat raced, he hadn't completed many gym tests, and on bowside he wasn't really the oarsman he was meant to be. It was as hard for him as it was for McDonald, and just as Topolski was the only one prepared to sympathise with McDonald, Clark's real friends sympathised and tried to protect Clark so that he could get on his feet again.

He returned after Christmas reluctantly, and was immediately greeted by the prospect of a 5,000m ergometer test. Having flown in at four o'clock that afternoon, the prospect of doing an ergometer at 9am the following day, jetlag and all, did little to encourage him. He felt that it was stupid to do the test with jetlag, but knew he had to because he hadn't done one yet, and Topolski had made it clear that he would not wait any longer. The other Americans, who had also arrived late to the training camp, were excused this particular test. The test would be unlikely to produce a representative score, but Clark had arrived two days late to the camp, and I can only assume it was a chance for Topolski to lay down his authority. The pressure was on. The test ergometer, followed by his first outing in a less then perfect Four, led to the 'soup throwing incident', an outburst of temper which led to a cup of vegetable soup decorating the wall of a London Rowing Club changing room. It was a vivid demonstration of his frustration. 'It's no good: I just can't row on bowside, I want to change back to strokeside,' he told Topolski. Topolski wouldn't have it. He was fed up with Clark not abiding by his wishes. Incidents like this are not unusual, particularly at selection time, but they are always remembered. I doubt that this is the only story that Topolski remembers from his many years coaching and rowing, but at the time it didn't seem so funny. However, the outburst did the trick, for the next week Clark was mercifully back on strokeside, where he was comfortable and could finally redeem himself as a first-class oarsman, and more importantly re-establish his own self-confidence and enjoyment of the sport that he had forgotten how to love.

Topolski denies ever putting Clark back on strokeside; he claims to have been distracted by the other crew who were racing London University. Topolski states: 'Clark paddled off on strokeside, a fact I only noticed later on in the day . . . I decided that I could not at that moment face yet another fight with him. I neglected to go and confront him over the very issue that should have been central to him being allowed back into the squad.'

In the following week, Clark demonstrated that putting him back on to strokeside was a major decision which Topolski should have made weeks before. He was immediately comfortable, and started to perform at the level he knew he could. Unfortunately, however, Clark's sudden change in performance was not such good news for McDonald. Once he started to perform well, those who had rowed with both McDonald and Clark had no doubts that Clark would be taking the fourth seat on strokeside, which would leave McDonald on the bank. All that needed to happen now was for Clark to prove his worth.

Regardless of what had happened before Christmas, Clark was back on form. Rowing with the Isis boys, he was a tower of strength. He encouraged them, pushed them and coached them from within the crew to such an extent that they out-performed even their own hopes. They were impressed, and Topolski was surprised but relieved. Between the two of them, relationships had been strained for quite a while, and Topolski had become more and more convinced that any problem which cropped up anywhere in the squad was somehow caused by Clark's frustrating behaviour. Certainly, his attitude hadn't helped anybody, and Topolski's very obvious frustration with Clark had started to rub off on the squad. Clark had become Topolski's scapegoat. Clark knew this; he told Lyons before Christmas that he believed he was 'living on borrowed time', and nobody could blame Topolski for his aggression toward Clark: it is a nuisance to have a good oarsman under-performing and unhappy.

With Clark now content and performing well on strokeside, the pressures in the squad changed. Clark was more confident, and so too were Pelham and Ward: with Clark back on strokeside, they could now fight for the last bowside seat. Clark promised them he wasn't going back on to bowside, and they all agreed it made sense. Now that the atmosphere was more relaxed, Topolski eased up on Clark. Once again feeling in control, Topolski quickly got on with the rest of the trials; he was anxious to try to finalise a crew. The weather didn't help matters: it was appalling, the coldest January on record. Topolski loved to see his oarsmen battle against the elements, and whilst other oarsmen returned to the comforts of the gym and land training, he kept his crews out on the water. Every day saw them out in the freezing wind, sleet and ice, conquering any conditions the Tideway threw at them. The oarsmen hated it. That kind of cold is relentless, it bites through any clothing you wear to combat it. The Americans in particular thought it was madness, but under protest they all followed Topolski's instructions, and persevered.

Battling through harsh winter conditions is a modern oarsman's trend; it's as if there is some kind of bravado in beating the conditions, and, crazy as it may seem, there is something to be achieved from not being put off by rough water and harsh conditions. It teaches you respect for the waves and the skilled boatmanship which racing a Boat

Race on the Tideway requires, and in Topolski's eyes it was the ideal way to make the fighters he was after.

On the coldest day of the year, indeed of the decade, Wednesday, 14 January, Topolski once again set out two Fours for seat racing. He picked McDonald and Gleeson for the strokes, Lyons and Cadoux-Hudson opposite in the three seats, Clark and Huntington in the two seats, and the rivals Ward and Pelham bringing up the bows. It was, to say the least, an odd line-up. Topolski obviously was considering Clark for the Blue Boat again, because these were all potential Blue Boat crew members. Yet if he was to race Clark, would it not seem crazy to compare him with the best strokesider in the squad, Huntington, particularly as Topolski said he wasn't even thinking of putting him back into the first boat? It would have made more sense to race him against Gleeson or McDonald, or even Stewart. Lyons and Cadoux-Hudson were obvious swaps, because they were supposedly the best two bowside rowers. The Seat Race was a bit of a farce, because they all knew who was going to be raced, and secrecy is of prime importance in seat racing. A tossing, pitching rough day on the Tideway is not the fairest of places to assess differences in performance of two men; bad steering by the cox, or a wave that hits one crew and not the other, will be enough to alter the result by four or five seconds. The results of the first two races left Cadoux-Hudson a length faster than Lyons over a seven-minute race. Neither oarsman read much into this result, except for noting that Cadoux-Hudson was good in the rough conditions and that both men felt thoroughly fed up with Topolski for putting them through this senseless farce. Topolski then tried to swap Clark and Huntington, but the racing had to be abandoned, as the water was too rough to continue. Jon Fish, the American cox, remembered this as a typical example of Topolski's paranoia about always training, no matter what the conditions were like, and no matter what state his oarsmen were in. 'The Boat Race is different and treacherous, and will demand more from you than you can imagine,' Topolski would repeat. Training in those conditions was not fruitful, it was dangerous. And although they went out they didn't stay out for long, thus wasting what could have been a useful session training on the ergometers. This was yet another example of the gap that existed between coach and oarsmen, and put the Americans into the focal point of contention when it came to disagreeing with Topolski's decisions. Clark was again the centre of attention in a dispute, although Huntington had spoken out loudly in protest at the ridiculous nature of the trials. Lack of trust between crew and coach was creeping in again.

The next two days were spent training indoors, the weather and water too wild to make outings worthwhile. But the approaching weekend saw the crews back afloat, this time on the relative calm of the Thames in Henley. Their two-week training camp on the Tideway, thankfully, had come to an end. It had been an illusory two weeks. Clark had gone from being on the verge of giving up with himself, the Boat Race and rowing in Britain, to a return to form and a refiring of his motivation, due to Topolski at last recognising Clark's need to row strokeside, and putting him with the Isis squad as a chance to prove it. The result led to what Isis coach, Jeff Jacobs, described as 'the best Isis he'd ever coached', a crew jump-started by Clark performing with the power and presence only a true International can do. Topolski, aware of Clark's improvement, had started to test him for a seat in the Blue Boat on strokeside, thus giving McDonald an edgy feeling that now it was his neck on the line, and not that of Pelham and Ward. It was irritating for McDonald to see someone who outwardly had tried so little and given himself and the coaches so much emotional grief suddenly become an arch rival for the seat that meant so much to him. Mcdonald vowed to his squad that Clark would have to beat him very publicly to get his seat; his intention was never to let him have that chance, and having the close friendship of Topolski was helping him in that ambition.

8

Saturday, 17 January, 1987, was the day that McDonald was to be seat raced against Clark., Being President, McDonald had the advantage of knowing which of them was to be seat raced that day, and Clark and he came high on the list. Both Clark and McDonald had so far got off lightly, but the race had to happen as there had to be some sort of comparison between the two of them. Foreknowledge of the race didn't give McDonald much peace of mind, although he wrote in his diary that evening that he was not scared of being beaten by Clark. He said it would be a close race, but he was sure that he could win as long as Clark had no outside help. McDonald was worried that Clark's friends would cheat to ensure that Clark beat McDonald. (Why he thought that any member of the squad would particularly want to rig such a critical race so that the slowest person would win, I'm not sure.)

Cheating in a Seat Race doesn't do anybody any good; if the wrong person gets selected, it just makes the end crew go slower. McDonald's thoughts highlight his lack of confidence in his ability to beat Clark. He said it would be a hard race, and was obviously not as confident as he tried to convince himself that he was; the majority of the crew on the other hand were confident of Clark, because since Christmas he had been rowing very well indeed. The bets were on him, and it certainly hadn't crossed their minds that he might need a helping hand. Clark was confident that he could beat McDonald; he had asked for a chance to beat him, and being given that chance, he was determined to prove himself.

The two Fours for the Seat Race were announced as

Gleeson, Hull, Clark and Ward, with Fish coxing, and Penney, Cadoux-Hudson, McDonald and Pelham, with Lobbenburg coxing. They were to race from the Henley Royal Regatta course backwards from the finish post downstream to the start at the end of Temple Island, approximately a seven-minute race, 2,200m long. None of the crew members except McDonald knew the format of the racing. McDonald knew, because he was President and had access to that information from Topolski. Seat racing relies on a degree of secrecy: if none of the crew know who is being raced, or at what stage they will be swapped into another crew, then there is no temptation for anyone to save their energy for the races that affect them personally. If this happened, one particular race would inevitably affect the results of another person's race. Complete secrecy is in practice difficult to achieve because, by this stage of selection, there are some obvious races which the coaches will want to try. A great deal of honesty is therefore crucial to good seat racing, and trust that the oarsmen want the best men in the final line-up.

Topolski almost certainly would not have been looking forward to these trials; his close relationship with McDonald must have left him wanting McDonald to come out of the racing on top, but he knew that Clark was likely to perform well. Had the oarsmen allowed it, he probably would not have raced Clark against McDonald, but he had little option: Clark was training hard and looking good, and the other oarsmen wanted to see McDonald trialled against Clark. It had been a long winter, and he would be relieved when selection was over; the oarsmen would be, too. An air of expectation and urgency clung as both crews prepared to race. Like thoroughbreds, they jostled for places on the landing stage, keen to get started with the business of the day.

Starting the first race, Topolski called the crews level and gave the signal. The boats surged forward oblivious to everything around them. Heads up, eyes forward and staring, ears tuned to the driving calls of their coxswain. Each man kicks on his stretcher, concentration focused on the end of his blade, giving every last ounce of his strength. Gleeson's boat won by about a length and a half. Pelham's stretcher broke halfway through the race, which, Topolski decided, probably explained the big difference between the two crews. The second race saw Ward and Pelham swapped, the two rivals having another chance to prove their worth. In this race the two crews drew equal, leaving Ward the winner by a length and a half, a significant turnabout since the shorter Seat Races at Thorpe Park in December, where Pelham had beaten Ward twice. This second race was also the first part of the McDonald versus Clark race. It is interesting to note that if McDonald had worried about losing to Clark and had saved himself in the first race, it would explain Ward's spectacular improvement over his Christmas results, as Ward would have been helped along by McDonald not rowing flat out in the first race, in order to save himself for his own trial, which included the second race of the Pelham versus Ward trial. Nobody knows whether that did happen, but since McDonald obviously thought cheating possible in Seat Races, it wouldn't have been beyond him to do so. Ward and Pelham probably seemed unimportant to him at that stage.

The third race was the one they all waited for. Clark and McDonald swapped seats, and the crews paddled back to the start. McDonald should by now have an advantage over Clark because Clark was supposedly not in as good a shape as the rest of the squad, and would therefore be feeling the effects of the first two seven-minute rows. A seven-minute race is short enough to have the oarsmen working anaerobically, a process of energy formation which builds up lactic acid, the poison which causes the rapid muscle fatigue associated with sprinting. Good fitness and strength increases the amount of time the athlete can tolerate performing anaerobically. If Clark was not as fit as the others, he would be suffering the effects of lactic acid build-up in his legs.

The race began, Clark's crew leaping forward immediately more powerfully than their opponents. After a minute they had taken a length, after four minutes they had clear water, and their rhythm and boat speed was obviously superior to McDonald's crew. 'The difference in the two crews was so great,' remembered Penney, 'that it surprised us all. We expected Clark to be better than McDonald, but this was a joke!' Four and half minutes, and they were still moving away. Then things started to go wrong. Topolski called to Penney to lower his stroke rate. His rate was thirty-two, the agreed cadence for the race, but Topolski wanted them down. Penney lowered the rate as they swept towards the Island. 'It didn't matter anymore because Clark had won, we were a long way ahead and comfortable rowing at that pace. We still had more to give, but because Topolski called again and again for the rate to come down, I took the rate down again, then the power came down too, until we were rowing light pressure. Of course, once we were rowing light, McDonald's crew started to gain, they were still rowing flat out. As we drew alongside the Island, it was obvious that Topolski wasn't going to stop the race, they drew alongside us, so, disobeying Topolski's demands, we picked up, racing the last half-minute to the finish. McDonald's crew were sprinting for the line as if the race was still on. To our amazement, Topolski didn't even stop the race at the end of the Island. Instead, it carried for a further minute downstream to the gate. By the time he called the race to a halt, we were still leading by just over half a length, but there was a great deal of confusion in the crew.'

McDonald's crew thought that they had pulled back their opposition in the last two minutes. they were oblivious to the messing around that had gone on in the middle of the race because, being behind, they hadn't been able to see Clark's crew rowing practically light pressure. When Topolski announced the result of the race as a win to Clark by a quarter of a length, Clark's crew were horrified. To coin a phrase, said Clark, 'you can't be serious!' Clark had won fair and square, he had annihilated McDonald, but Topolski wasn't letting on. He completely avoided the issue of calling the rates down and the fact that Clark's crew had practically stopped rowing when he had repeatedly demanded that they bring the rate down. 'It was like some kind of practical joke,' said Clark, but it wasn't very funny. The other crew wasn't too aware of what the problem was, and Penney's crew just sat with their mouths open unable to believe that Topolski wasn't going to admit that Clark had beaten McDonald.

As a cox you can tell a lot during a Seat Race. Some oarsmen get into the crew and slot straight in, others get in and take over, and some upset the crew completely and need all the help the cox can give to get into the swing. The really good ones are the ones who take over, instil their rhythm and power and dominate the crew, so the race is theirs. For the ones who upset the crew there is little chance, they get in and the crew falls apart. 'McDonald,' said Fish 'was one of the unfortunate ones: when he got in to Gleeson's Four the crew fell apart. In his own desperation to win he pulled the crew apart, and Gleeson didn't have the strength or the experience to stop him.' Fish is an experienced cox with a lot of Seat Races under his belt; the Americans use seat racing for selection more than the British. With all his experience he was well qualified to quickly assess any changes when seats were swapped, and he knew that the information he provided to the new combination could help them a lot to quickly gel as a crew. McDonald had been lucky to have Fish for that race: a less experienced cox might not have carried on regardless of the comments flying between Penney and Topolski, but Fish was a professional immersed in making his crew win. As they drew nearer to the other crew, he had urged his crew on, encouraging them to up the rate and sprint for the finish, distracting them from everything except thoughts of racing back through the other crew. Fish pushed his crew and kept them focused until they were given the signal to stop; only then did he let himself question why the other crew had slowed down before the finish.

Out on the water, Topolski wouldn't listen to any complaints: he didn't want to stop there, and he turned the crews around, swapped Clark with Cadoux-Hudson and put Tony Ward in Clark's seat on strokeside. Having raced Clark on strokeside, he wanted to see if Clark really could row on bowside or not. If he put up a good performance on bowside, the result of the previous race would be irrelevant. They paddled to the start and set off again; they were tired, but all of them were fuelled and fired to fight any battle anyone cared to set up for them. It was a good psychological ploy from Topolski. Royle told me that both he and

Topolski were convinced that Clark could row technically well on bowside, but because he still felt uncertain he hadn't yet performed up to standard on his new side. His psychology was preventing him performing, and if they could overcome that then they could put him in to the Blue Boat on bowside. Royle felt that he would only need one good result to give him confidence on bowside, and they hoped that he would perform well against Cadoux-Hudson, which would give him a boost. Clark always performs better when he's a happy man and, having just beaten McDonald, he was just so. If he was ever going to perform well on bowside, it was now. However, if he was beaten badly it would work the other way and reaffirm his lack of skill on bowside.

Both crews jumped off the start, settling quickly to a stroke rate of thirty-two, challenging each other for the lead. Clark's crew were finding it difficult to keep to the rate, and it was now his turn to rattle the crew. He ruined any chance they had of holding a lead, and they were rudely reminded of Clark's lack of bowside ability which was still rough and disruptive to the rhythm and speed of the boat. Cadoux-Hudson's crew took the lead after a minute and increased the gap between them at every stroke. They won by nearly two lengths; the result confirmed to everybody that without a doubt Clark was better on strokeside.

Back in the warmth and splendour of the Leander Club, Topolski, McDonald and Royle gathered together to discuss the afternoon's races whilst the rest of the squad put the boats away and showered and changed ready for the drive back to Oxford. Discussion of the afternoon's racing was inevitably subdued as they waited for Topolski to confirm the results and make a decision about the two crews. What would be his next move? In the minds of the crew the selection decisions were straightforward; McDonald would have to stand down from the crew, Clark had publicly demonstrated his superiority on strokeside and thus vindicated his place in the crew. Bowside would be Lyons, Cadoux-Hudson, Hull and Ward. But they were worried that the President wouldn't accept the decision. The question remained: would the President do the honourable thing and stand down as other Presidents had done before him? Quintus Travis, the Cambridge President of 1985, stood down from the crew but remained in charge of the day-to-day running of the club and took his glory from watching the crew from the bank. As far as he was concerned, the honour lay in producing the fastest crew, and when he was beaten, he stood down. Prince Edward, then a student at Cambridge and thus aware of the desirous prestige and honour associated with rowing in the Blue Boat, said he was filled 'with admiration when, as President of the University Boat Club, he sacrificed his own ambition for the sake of the team.'

Before they left Henley that Saturday, Topolski called Clark into the boathouse and told him that he was satisfied with Clark's behaviour and the way he was rowing. He said that the day's racing had demonstrated that he was at last getting fit and should now return to train as part of the potential Blue Boat, and that he would be rowing on bowside. Clark was subdued in disbelief. He said Topolski was acting as if Clark had been on trial to demonstrate his fitness and good behaviour, and that it didn't matter who he had beaten. It was as if he should be glad of the leniency shown to him, as if Topolski was doing him a favour. What could he say? He could not voice his thoughts and left with a shrug of his shoulders, knowing that Topolski and McDonald had overstepped their mark. Personal likes and dislikes are irrelevant in crew selection: it is meant to be a decision based purely on ability. So why was McDonald in the crew, when he'd just been publicly defeated? Why was Clark back on bowside when he had demonstrated so many times his inability to adapt to rowing on that side? And what about Tony Ward? Clark had promised Ward and Pelham that he would prove he was better than them before accepting a place on bowside, and Topolski had promised to give them a chance to beat him. Clark wondered what he could say to them. McDonald shouldn't be in the crew; they had proven that today, or so he thought. Obviously Topolski's interpretation of the races was different to his and the nine other men's, McDonald excluded. It wasn't until later on that week that they heard Topolski's interpretation of the races: Topolski and McDonald said that the Seat Race proved nothing, because Penney hadn't rowed flat out in the first race when McDonald was in his crew, thus giving Clark an advantage. In the second race, they accused Penney of over-rating the other crew; they said that only when he finally lowered the rate in response to Topolski's demand was the race fair, and at that point McDonald's crew had pulled back, thus demonstrating his superiority over Clark. The Seat Races were thus, he said, inconsequential, and could only be used to demonstrate that Clark was at last beginning to try and was perhaps worthy of a place in the crew. Hence he was asked to row on bowside, 'the weaker side in the crew'.

How two races could possibly be interpreted so differently by people in the same team, supposedly working toward the same goal, remained a mystery to many coaches and oarsmen who heard about the trials. It is difficult, perhaps almost impossible, to get laboratory-like conditions in trials such as these. Honesty and clarity are the main requirements for successful seat racing, and it seemed that there was little of either at these trials. Both sides left with the belief that the other had been out to cheat on the results. There is no other evidence available about these Seat Race trials, only the word of Topolski and McDonald against the word of the nine crew members. The only thing that is clear is that Clark's crew, with Penney at stroke, crossed the finish line first. How you wish to interpret the result will depend upon whose word you value most.

Whatever your interpretation, Clark returned to Oxford that day with the knowledge that his return to bowside would not go down well, particularly with Tony Ward and Hugh Pelham, who would now not be considered for the last place on bowside because Clark had switched sides again. It was just three weeks after Christmas, and suddenly Clark's doubts about the Boat Race, Topolski and McDonald had returned. He was beginning to tire of his rowing days at Oxford.

Coaches Steve Royale and Daniel Topolski. Topolski was Oxford's chief coach for fifteen years. Royale, previously part-time Oxford coach, became professional manager upon Topolski's retirement.

Coach Mike Spracklen, OBE, and President Donald McDonald. Spracklen now coaches the Canadian National rowing team, although he still returns annually to coach Oxford for a couple of weeks.

Christopher Clark – scapegoat for the 1987 Boat Race dispute. Member of US Team 1985.

Daniel Lyons – partner to Clark in Coxless Pairs (1985) and Gold medallist in Coxless Fours (1986). Lyons is now a professional rowing coach to the US Naval Academy.

Tony Ward – Oxford oarsman who sacrificed the honour of a Blue in 1986 and was prepared to again in 1987 until he realized a lesser man would take his place.

Jon Fish – US Cox to Bronze Medal Four (1985) and Bronze Medal Eight (1986). Fish never realized his dream to cox the Boat Race, but returned to Oxford in 1988 to help the new President Penney instigate the changes and see justice done.

The final 1987 Boat Race crew (left to right), Bow: Pelham, 2. Gish, 3. Ward, 4. Gleeson, 5. Hull, 6. McDonald, 7. Cadoux-Hudson, 8. Stewart, Cox: Gruselle.

9

'Hello, Tony, Donald here.' Tony Ward waited to hear what his President had to say. He had been awaiting a call from McDonald or Topolski confirming the news that he was no longer wanted for the Blue Boat: Clark had told him the news that Topolski had put him back on bowside earlier that evening. McDonald wasted no breath over the call: he told Ward that the day's results indicated that he wasn't good enough to row in the Blue Boat, and that he would be rowing in Isis. He didn't pause to explain why this decision had been made, or to give Tony a chance to ask any questions: his message was short and clear. Ward was no longer in the crew. He was livid, as he felt McDonald was using him to further his own ends. McDonald had said so often that he wouldn't be happy about Clark rowing instead of him, because 'he'd trained so hard, and Clark hadn't'. But when he was beaten fairly and squarely, he wasn't prepared to let the same ethos stand for others. 'I'd trained hard too, but that didn't seem to matter,' Ward told me.

Ward telephoned Gavin after McDonald's call, needing some support. Gavin was horrified that Ward was being made to pay because McDonald and Topolski hadn't proved that McDonald was better than Clark. There was no doubt in his mind that Clark shouldn't be rowing on bowside, and that Tony shouldn't be left out because of this rivalry between McDonald and Clark. They had all been rowing together for some months now, and it was painfully obvious from inside the squad who made the boat go faster. On strokeside Clark was better than McDonald, and on bowside Tony was better than Clark.

The trouble was that Topolski didn't want to know, and was refusing to acknowledge that Clark was performing well now. He'd given Clark a chance mainly because he had been forced to by his oarsmen. Clark had taken this chance, but for some reason Topolski wasn't prepared to acknowledge the result. To 'Anon' in *The Guardian,* the oarsmen were right to question their coach: 'The coach dominates at lower levels, but at this level many people know more from sitting inside the crew than watching from the outside. . . It's all about making boats move.' It is difficult for the coaches to stay unbiased during selection, and this was particularly true of Topolski, who had a great relationship with McDonald but not with many of the rest of the squad, particularly Clark. There was no doubt Topolski had grown closer to McDonald during the year; McDonald had always been the one to ask Topolski to continue coaching when the going got tough, and he had acted supportively during all the arguments about training. Topolski must have felt a deep sense of loyalty and friendship to him, and their friendship clearly meant that pure boat speed was no longer the primary issue. Gavin felt that they needed to make a stand, particularly for Ward, who had already lost one Blue and who shouldn't lose another just because McDonald's ego couldn't accept being beaten by Clark, who hadn't even been training hard until the last few weeks. 'Donald was protecting himself and Topolski was protecting Donald, for some reason,' Gavin said, 'and innocent parties like Tony were being made to pay, and that was not fair.'

That evening, an informal get-together between the members of the potential Blue Boat led to a rather rash decision. Having decided that they needed to act quickly with regard to McDonald's proposed plan to drop Ward, they rang Topolski to talk directly with him. They needed to ask him to explain the decision and to tell him that they really weren't happy with it. Unfortunately, a British Telecom telephone strike meant they never managed to get hold of Topolski. Knowing that they were unlikely to see Topolski for a while because they were due to be coached by Spracklen for the next two weeks, they decided they would have to ring McDonald instead and tell him that they were dissatisfied, that the seat race was unfair, and that they wanted the selection process to continue. They had wanted to talk to Topolski first because they felt sure that McDonald wouldn't be interested in putting himself through selection again, but they needn't have worried: they couldn't get hold of McDonald either. Instead, they arranged to meet in Oriel Square at the normal time of 1pm, agreeing that they could talk to McDonald there. Lyons and Hull were appointed spokesmen for the crew, and agreed to take McDonald to Lyons's room and talk to him there. The meeting didn't go quite as planned.

They were correct in their assumption that McDonald wouldn't be interested in what they had to say, and he was understandably on the defensive. Their friendly chat quickly turned into a fruitless argument, in which neither party was clear of where to go next; Lyons and Hull were asking for selection to continue and decisions to be explained, McDonald quite clearly felt that his position in the crew was being threatened, as was his authority as President. Richard Hull detailed the meeting clearly: 'There is no easy way to tell somebody that you don't want to row with them. McDonald knew something was up before he arrived, because he'd arranged for a spare oarsman to be available to row in Isis. He was on the defensive from the moment he arrived. We tried to lead him into a discussion and explain clearly why we didn't agree with Saturday's results and the decisions he and Dan had made, but he didn't want to listen.'

Lyons says that McDonald completely ignored Hull, 'which was unnecessary'. And he ignored what they were trying to tell him. 'He jumped to the subject of Clark and the fastest crew and who'd trained the hardest, and kept saying he was the President and it was up to him.' After fifteen minutes, he stood up and left, saying: 'We're not getting anywhere.' They all left in the van, McDonald having said they'd better go to Marlow without him, so they took him back to his home in Botley, and set off to Marlow for their outing. What was supposed to be a quiet meeting had resulted in them leaving the President at home with the harsh realisation that the crew weren't prepared to row with him as things stood. Fish spelt out the problem: 'The format is that he was President, so it was his decision, but if he wanted to row he'd have to do so alone until he agreed to some proper trials.' They had no idea of the consequences of their action, but they guessed there would have to be more trials and thought maybe McDonald might stand down. Most people could not tolerate so much animosity and disbelief in their ability, and certainly would not want to be in a crew with seven other people who thought that they shouldn't be there. 'If I was in his shoes, I'd have been questioning my own ability, not only to row but also to lead,' Ward remarked.

They left him at home, as he asked them to, to sort something out. For now, they were happy to be without him, and they drove on to Marlow for their outing with Spracklen.

McDonald had relinquished his position in the crew, and they waited for him to contact them with some details of further trials. They hadn't considered any further action themselves; they just carried on naively for three days, training as a crew and enjoying every minute of it. They heard nothing from McDonald or from Topolski. They knew Spracklen had been instructed by McDonald to continue coaching the crew until he contacted him again, and Mike was happy to abide by the President's request. The only person who knew anything about McDonald's plans was the OUBC Secretary, Hugh Pelham, who successfully abstained from taking sides during the ensuing dispute, principally, others said, because he was Secretary, and because of the advice offered to him by his father, an ex-Oxford oarsman, who had been involved in a Boat Race dispute in 1959. He had been a 'mutineer', and had lost his Blue because of it. Clearly his advice was to carry on rowing and steer clear of the politics, and Hugh's abstension, along with his amiable character, allowed him to run a double act, fielding information to McDonald about the crew whenever he asked for it, and passing information to the crews about McDonald whenever they asked. For the time being, McDonald was the only one asking Pelham for information, and, happy to oblige, he told McDonald that the crew was training, content to wait until they heard from him. They had no plans to do anything else. McDonald's lack of contact should have been disconcerting to them, but they didn't read it as the lull before the storm that it turned out to be; while they trained, McDonald was busy plotting how to get himself back into the crew and Clark out for good. He was gathering support, not for his ability as an oarsman, but for his power as President. As President, authority over the crews and selection, instruction and direction of Boat Club members was entirely in his control: the OUBC Constitution said so.

Section C: 1 – The OUBC Constitution

The President's responsibilities are to:

> 'select and manage all University crews, to preside at all Captain's Meetings and meetings of the Committee, and to act as final judge in all questions pertaining to the interpretation of the constitution.'

McDonald went as far as to seek legal advice from an old London Rowing Club friend and lawyer. He wanted an exact interpretation of the Boat Club Constitution and to know the limits of his authority. He was duly assured that the President's power, according to the Constitution, was total. It was, as Lyons said, 'a Constitution even Napoleon would have been proud of!' Once assured of the safety of his Presidency, he turned to a great number of advisers, most of them Old Blues who had no knowledge of this year's crew but were prepared to offer their advice on how the President should manage a rebellious squad who were challenging his authority, which is how he presented the problem to them. He presumed that the Americans were protecting Ward so that Clark could get a place in the crew, and he was very motivated to regain his command so that his place in the crew would not be lost. He referred to the Clark/Ward issue as a 'marriage of convenience', in which he saw himself as the scapegoat and was outraged at the indignity of their action. He wanted to row in the crew and was going to make sure he did; outrage and disbelief seemed to be his main motivation for reacting so quickly and violently to the meeting in Lyons's room. His movements from here onwards were always guarded, and were planned to secure himself a position in the crew. He was to charge the Americans with trying to take over the Boat Club.

Did he never stop to wonder why they did not want him in the crew? Was he not horrified by the animosity of his fellow rowers? And if he was so sure of his position in the crew, why wasn't he prepared to demonstrate his superiority over Clark and make Clark demonstrate his superiority over Tony Ward? These were questions that Ward, Hull, Lyons, Penney and all the other oarsmen who were involved would ask themselves and every other individual who was to accuse them of behaving outrageously over the next few weeks.

McDonald chose the story that the Americans had 'taken over the Boat Club and no longer required him as President', and he spent the three days while the crew trained drumming up support, not from his crewmates, but from old Blues and senior members of the University Boat Club. The two crews, who were still training, had no idea what McDonald was up to. When they left him at home on Monday afternoon, they did so with the message that they weren't happy with the selection decisions and that they wanted more trials. They expected him to relay this message to Topolski; they certainly had no intention to 'take over the Boat Club' – nothing so premeditated had crossed their minds. They merely felt that, as members of the Oxford University Boat Club, they were entitled to pass opinion on the selection of the crew and the management of the Boat Club, both which they felt were being mishandled.

McDonald refused to tell me his story; however, immediately after the Boat Race in 1987, he was only too pleased to talk through his carefully-planned manoeuvres. He spoke to a number of people, friends and reporters, and it is from these sources that I relay his story to you.

His first move was to telephone Topolski and inform him of the crew's supposed 'takeover'. Topolski, quite understandably, was horrified and offered his full support. McDonald then called Ronnie Howard, Chairman of the President's Advisory Committee. Howard has an unfortunate history of being in the centre of two past Boat Race quarrels. The first and best remembered was when he was President in 1959, and the second was when he was coach in 1965.

Howard had been elected President in 1959, when Reed Rubin, an American oarsman who had rowed in the losing 1958 crew, had stood against him and the established Oxford Boat Race coach of that era, Jumbo Edwards. Rubin and five others from the 1958 crew wanted to make changes to the training methods and the technique which the Oxford Boat Club used, but to do this he wanted to relieve Jumbo Edwards of his command and have Jim Rathschmidt from Yale to be in charge of coaching, and he wanted Jumbo to act under him. The circumstances of this quarrel were quite different from the one McDonald had on his hands. This dispute started well before Howard's election to President; Rubin and the other five mutineers hoped to start their proposed changes by getting Rubin elected as President, and to do so he and Grimes (another American) financed an unsuccessful campaign after the 1958 Boat Race. At that time, the Blues in residence did not get to vote in the new President; his election was entirely the job of the College Captains. 'We should have been more like politicans in our campaigning,' Rubin told me. 'Ronnie was well known and liked by the College Captains, and they couldn't really see why he shouldn't be President. They were wary of someone with new ideas, particularly as he was a foreigner.' Ronnie Howard was elected. Rather than accept Ronnie as President and join in the Oxford University Boat Club under Jumbo Edwards, Rubin, Grimes and Dave Edwards (Jumbo's son), the OUBC Secretary M. J. W. Hall and S. Douglas-Mann formed their own crew with three others and suggested a race-off against Ronnie's crew. The winner, they said, should be the one to race Cambridge on Boat Race day. They refused to join Howard and

Jumbo Edwards's ranks because they disagreed with the method of technique and training which Jumbo coached. The establishment was horrified, and a fierce battle ensued, involving the coaches and old Blues who felt that the English tradition of the Boat Race was under threat. 'It became a national incident,' Rubin told me. 'The atmosphere was grim. particularly since we weren't even challenging the Boat Race or tradition; this was a sporting argument.' Unlike the quarrel McDonald was experiencing now, in 1959 Rubin and Grimes had carefully plotted their challenge against Howard. They wanted to directly challenge Oxford's techniques and training methods, which does not seem so surprising when you consider the arguments which were rife in the rowing world at that time. Everyone was arguing about which technique to row and which were the best methods to train the crew. Oxford was the perfect setting for a dispute, because they had just suffered sixteen consecutive losses in the Boat Race. Rubin's rebel crew never did get the opportunity to race the University crew as the power of the old Blues made sure their efforts were wasted. Once they realised there was no chance of racing off against Jumbo's crew, Rubin's lot stopped trying, some of them returning to row with the University and to win the Boat Race. The win was portrayed nationally as a lesson against rebellion, and a win for the Establishment that had supported Howard and Jumbo.

Howard's second little head-to-head with the Boat Race had nothing to do with the crew members but had a lot to do with saving the face of the Establishment. Howard was part of a two-man coaching team, the other coach being Sam McKenzie, the well-known Australian sculler and practical joker. McKenzie was renowned for winning the Diamond Sculls at Henley no less than six times. Shortly before starting his stint as coach, McKenzie was withdrawn from the coaching team because of a scandal about a joke letter which McKenzie was reported to have written to one of the potential crew member's fathers. The crew, particularly its four Yale oarsmen, were not amused by McKenzie's withdrawal, as McKenzie was a highly sought-after coach and fierce competitor. In reference to his withdrawal, McKenzie told the Press: 'Oxford seemed in trouble with their Englishness,' a statement which would have held particularly true for the abhorrent ending of the 1987 dispute. This little dispute ended fairly amicably, but it seems symbolic that once again Howard played a part in saving the face of the Establishment against a foreigner.

McDonald had picked the perfect bait for drumming up support from old Blues. Nothing riles an Englishman more than the threat of takeover by a bunch of foreigners, and Howard was the perfect ally. He undoubtedly considered himself rather knowledgeable when it came to winning a mutiny led by American oarsmen, and was the perfect person to start with. Upon hearing McDonald's plight, he offered his full support and advice. His first gem was to tell McDonald to make sure he had full support of all his coaches, and to make sure he got to them before the Americans did. The best way to do that was to keep his next move quiet, let the crew think he was in a quandary, and that he was rethinking his position, letting them think that their complaints had been heard. Howard advised him to call a meeting with all the OUBC coaches as soon as possible.

By the end of the next day, McDonald had the support of the most 'influential' of the Oxford senior members: Michael Barry, Senior Treasurer; Mike Pelham, 1959 mutineer and a member of the Oxford University Trust Fund; Dick Fishlock, old Blue and Chairman of the Oxford University Trust Fund; and Ronnie Howard, President in 1959, who had put down the mutiny crew of that year. These four individuals see themselves as guardians of the Boat Race, and indeed do play an important role in organising sponsorship and safeguarding the long-term needs of the Boat Club.

McDonald had also enlisted the help of his brother, Captain Hugh McDonald, a member of the elite Ninth Parachute Squadron, and of Simon Barker, an old London Rowing Club friend and practising barrister. With every telephone call, he received more and more advice on how to effect a complete recapture of the Boat Club and total authority over every oarsman who wanted to row in the Boat Race that year. His plan was to give them no choice but to agree to everything he set down as the law.

McDonald had been clever: he had chosen to cause a stir and make the problems of the Boat Club public by announcing that there was a rebellion going on which was undermining the University and its success story, the Boat Race, He didn't know how to regain favour with the crew, but demonstrated that he was quite capable of showing his authority and generating support from many important Boat Race guardians. The 'crew mutiny' was a drama they understood, and once they knew his problem, they scripted an heroic strategy for him to follow. His strength to relentlessly pursue this strategy and maintain the dignity befitting an Oxford President came from the tremendous amount of support and advice he received; he was assured of his legal rights by his lawyer, Baker. He had a sea of tactical advice on battle co-ordination from a Squadron Leader and a mutiny-basher, and copious amounts of support for his morality from ex-Presidents who stood by his right to preside. He also had support as an oarsman from Topolski, who was prepared to give his word that McDonald was a better oarsman than Clark.

McDonald followed their advice and set the scene: 'Let them think they're in control,' they told him, so Hugh Pelham was employed to relay the message to the crew that McDonald was rethinking his position. 'Assure all outsiders who may have cause to stand on the side of the rebels that their action is their own, and nothing to do with your incompetence.' At a routine Captains' meeting that Wednesday evening, Topolski and Royle took the floor and announced the President's capability in dealing with such matters, reassurance that should have alerted Gavin Stewart, Vice-President and the only one of the existing crew who was present at the meeting. This statement was evidence that something ominous was about to happen.

'Be sure of your tactics, close all the gaps, make sure of your support and don't make a move until you are certain you can win, but most of all be firm,' was the advice that led to McDonald's full-bodied attempt to stamp his authority on the squad, once and for all.

10

The crew arrived at Marlow on Monday afternoon full of apologies and explanations for their lateness, which Mike Spracklen genially ignored; the Oxford boys weren't known for their time-keeping. Mike reduced his conversation with the crew to the basics, more concerned with ushering them into the boat and on to the water, as he was anxious to get the crew out for a paddle in what remained of the rapidly diminishing light. He noted McDonald's absence, but left questions as to his whereabouts until the end of the outing, when there would be time to talk. Finally boated and comfortable, the crew disappeared off down the Cookham stretch of the Thames, leaving Mike floundering in a launch that refused to start, which compounded his annoyance. There wasn't much light left and he had hoped to use this outing to settle the crew so that training could begin in earnest the following day. With this purpose in mind, he liked to be alongside the crew to note any problems with rigging or adjustment, and to point out the landmarks which would be helpful to the crew and cox whilst they were training.

His efforts to start the launch were finally rewarded just in time for him to meet and guide the crew back from Cookham Lock to the Marlow Scout Camp from where they were boating. It was only as they rounded the corner for the last four or five minutes of the row that Mike had time to relax and watch. Mike is at his best on the water alongside a crew. As the boat sweeps across the water, he absorbs every move and carefully breaks down each stroke of each blade to analyse its movement and precision, mentally noting the improvements that need to be made to increase the speed of the boat. This information he carefully stores, ready for retrieval at an appropriate point. As he watched them row, a plan for their improvement began to form in his mind. On the whole they looked quite good, demonstrating the prowess that one would expect from a crew with their combined experience. On a first outing one cannot always expect things to go well, but this crew looked happy and confident in themselves, and with a little work Mike felt that they would be a very fast crew.

As they drew alongside the landing stage and the cox called for 'Easy-oars', a hearty chatter broke out amongst the crew, always a good sign that the outing has gone well. Mike broke the conversation to ask the whereabouts of McDonald. He wasn't quite prepared for the answer that the crew gave him. They explained to him that they weren't happy about McDonald's crew selection, which had Clark rowing on bowside and had left Ward out. They explained to Mike that they had been unable to get in contact with Topolski, and so they had spoken directly to McDonald. They told him that the meeting had ended in unpleasant disagreement and that they had left McDonald in a fury back in Oxford, hopefully sorting out more trials. Mike accepted their explanation: he was there to coach, and wanted to do so without getting involved in arguments between crew members or the methods of selection. He expected to hear from McDonald later, and so asked no more questions. With the outing over, the crew left Marlow feeling tired but relaxed, content that Mike had been unruffled by their problems, and prepared to let the day's trauma rest until tomorrow.

That evening, Spracklen received an unexpected call from Topolski, informing him that the crew had 'kicked McDonald out', and that they had a serious problem on their hands. For Topolski to call Mike was very unusual. He would normally have very little contact with him during Mike's coaching stint. 'He was steamed up about the whole thing and talking about meetings and preventing things getting out of hand,' said Mike. Topolski asked him to attend a meeting of all the coaches, but Mike refused, explaining to him that he didn't want to get involved in a row, he just wanted to coach. Spracklen's involvement in the Boat Race has always been on a coaching level; he was never a student at Oxford and has few 'Old Blue' connections. Along with many other rowing enthusiasts, the Boat Race holds an interest for him because it is a part of his sport, and not because of the intrigue of the Varsity. The power structure and wheelings and dealings which were involved with the University were of little interest to him. Mike and Dan had been friends for several years, and Mike knew that Topolski was aware of these feelings. He hoped that he would respect his reasons for not wanting to get involved. Having had little contact with Topolski over the last few months, he found it hard to relate to the aggression which was streaming down the telephone line.

Later that evening, McDonald rang Spracklen to put in a personal plea for him to go to the meeting. He said he'd been badly treated by the rest of the squad. He told Spracklen that they had dropped him from the crew without reason. McDonald, like Topolski, seemed very fired up, and practically begged him to come to the meeting to support him. However, Spracklen felt in a quandary: he liked McDonald and wanted to be helpful, but he didn't want to get involved. He had plenty of experience of arguments over selection and knew that the atmosphere could get very tense. But he was concerned because he didn't really understand why McDonald and Topolski were so anxious to get him involved in what seemed to him to be a domestic dispute. Their actions and the tale he had been told didn't match the venom with which they spoke. He asked McDonald for some time to think; he would, he said, get back to him. With time to think, however, his feelings didn't change. He didn't want to get involved, and to him that meant not going to any meetings. When he rang back, he assured McDonald that he would act on his instructions, as President, but repeated that he wouldn't go to the meeting. The meeting therefore went ahead without him. As a result, Mike was asked by McDonald to continue coaching the crew that had boated that day until instructed otherwise.

If he had to get involved in any arguments between coaches and crew, Mike had a policy of always trying to understand the oarsman's complaint first, and if possible to stand on their side. Before the outing the next day, the conversation naturally revolved around the selection dilemma. The crew were looking for a solution, and were interested to hear Mike's opinion. Having listened intently to their discussions, it seemed to Mike that the oarsmen distrusted the selection decisions because the group believed that Tony Ward was being unfairly left out of the crew. They asked for Mike's opinion whether McDonald was a better oarsman than Chris Clark. In his opinion, said Mike, Clark was the better oarsman. But he realised that his opinion alone was not good enough, and that the current test results didn't clearly define who was the best. If they all felt strongly that McDonald shouldn't be in the crew because Clark was better on strokeside, they must obviously demonstrate Clark's superiority. They studied the best method to select between the two, appreciating that the current situation would make unbiased trials very difficult.

Mike could see that what was needed was a Seat Race in pairs between Clark and McDonald. He formulated a plan in his head which he thought might provide the answer. For his plan to work, he needed one oarsman who would rather row with McDonald than with Clark, and one who would rather row with Clark than McDonald, thus providing justification for both 'sides' to fight an even battle. But he felt that the chosen person should state themselves that they would rather row with one or the other, without knowing that he would then suggest a Seat Race in pairs. He knew Lyons would be happy to row with Clark, but who of equal ability would McDonald have confidence in? Out of the good bowside oarsmen, Tony Ward, Richard Hull and Tom Cadoux-Hudson, only Tom stood aloof from the fracas. He was one of the best oarsmen, and he had made it quite clear that he didn't have time to get involved in the dispute. Mike also knew he had not attended any of the meetings. When one also considered his experience of pairing with McDonald, he seemed the obvious partner. With this plan now worked out, Spracklen just had to get verification from Tom and from Dan Lyons that they would individually rather race McDonald and Clark respectively. He asked Tom first, who he would rather race with, McDonald or Clark; to this Tom replied, Clark! 'It rather took the wind out of my Seat Race plot,' Mike told me: there was no-one else in the squad of suitable ability who would rather pair with McDonald, and it seemed to him that the case was closed, and that Clark should be in the crew. But if they still wanted trials, the only thing he felt he could suggest was an ergometer test between the two, but they would have to discuss this between themselves. Spracklen never really gave consideration to the idea of Clark on bowside, because he said it was obvious that Clark had never really adapted to rowing there. The only further advice he proffered was that they should start their reconciliation by apologising to McDonald for the meeting in Lyons's room, and explain that they never meant to generate so much animosity. 'Most people will have a change of attitude after a sincere apology,' he told them.

Apart from that advice, he suggested nothing further. It was, he felt, their problem. He would only give his opinion if they asked him to answer a straight question, without prompting. The crew were not happy about Mike's disinclination to get involved, but understood and respected his stance. They were content for the moment, knowing that in his opinion Clark was the better oarsman, and hoped that he would act for them and lead their side of the argument, as Topolski was doing for McDonald. Spracklen was reluctant to take sides, and he gave them the same answer he had given to McDonald the previous evening when they asked him to act on their behalf: he said he would give answers to their questions, but he would not get involved in the decision-making. For now they had to be content knowing that Mike understood their plight and was prepared to carry on coaching them.

Content to continue training whilst they waited some contact from McDonald, they assumed they wouldn't have to wait long to hear from him, but they did get slightly worried by his three-day silence, particularly after the Captain's meeting on Wednesday evening, which Gavin reported back as being 'rather guarded'. McDonald and Topolski had been less than civil to Gavin, which had troubled him greatly. That, coupled with the rumours which were flying around Oxford about a 'mutiny' made them feel a little less comfortable about the silence. Time and time again they found that they had to explain themselves to their college friends and tutors. A lot of people were eager to know what was going on, but the truth was that they didn't really know themselves.

At about ten minutes to one, on Thursday, 22 January, the rowers began to head for Oriel Square in readiness for their daily departure to Marlow for their fourth outing with Spracklen. As everyone gathered in the Square, Richard Hull told them that McDonald had borrowed the van earlier in the day and hadn't yet returned, despite the fact that he knew that they needed it for the outing that afternoon. They suspected trouble. They were then met by Hugh Pelham who confirmed that McDonald still had the van, and that before their outing he wanted them all to go to the Vincent's Club for a meeting.

They didn't have to go far: Vincent's, the Oxford Sporting Blues Club, is situated on one of the side streets off Oriel Square, above the University outfitters. They all trooped in there behind Pelham, their shoddy rowing kit showing up starkly against the deep blue thick pile carpets. They walked up the stairs past pictures of all the great Oxford sportsmen, and as they did so, no doubt memories of a few 'wild' and raucous parties for which the club is famous crossed their minds! The stairs that lead off Oriel Square take you up two floors and past the bar before you get to the 'meeting room'. In the room sat McDonald, looking uncomfortable in a dark suit behind a big table. 'Rather overdressed for a rowing outing,' thought Clark. Topolski and Royle were there too, sat behind the table and looking even more uncomfortable than the President.

McDonald, true to form, wasted no time. He calmly and quietly announced to his fellow oarsmen that 'this was not a debate', he was there to read them a statement. There would be no discussion. He was only prepared to talk to individuals by phone after the meeting, if anyone cared to contact him. With that, he announced that there would be two new Boat Race crews, which were as follows:

> Crew A – Cox – Lobbenburg, Huntington, Hull, Penney, Cadoux-Hudson, Stewart, Pelham, McDonald, Ward.

Crew B – Cox – Gruselle, Gleeson, Baird, Gish, Ridgewell, Cheatle, Hill, Chinn, Race.

He asked all those oarsmen whose names had been announced to telephone him by twelve o'clock midnight and let him know whether or not they intended to row. His statement was clear: 'Call me if you want to row, if you don't somebody else will take your place.' He had the full support of the coaching team and backing of the University, he said, 'so this decision will stand'. He had left out Clark, Lyons and Fish from his crews because, as he later revealed, he saw them as the troublemakers in the Club and felt he could no longer work with them. His feelings that the oarsmen shouldn't be allowed to select the crew seemed to have vanished; it was because he couldn't work or row with Clark, Lyons or Fish that he had dropped them. In reality, he dropped them because he thought they were the only ones who would be prepared to fight the issue until the end. His interpretation of the depth of feeling in the squad was, however, mistakenly simplistic: Lyons and Fish may well have been the spokesmen and Clark a direct competitor for his seat, but they weren't the ones who were most determinedly driven by the morality of the whole issue. Stewart, Hull and Ward were equally adamant that the selection was biased and unfair, and, as the dispute deepened, Huntington and Penney grew more and more affected by the injustice that they were experiencing, and they were prepared to stand together.

As McDonald finished his piece the room filled with silence and blank expressionless faces. He had done as he had set out to do: his attack was a complete surprise. To finish, he gathered his papers, stood up and left the room without another word. Topolski and Royle followed him as loyal, attentive servants would follow their King; it seemed that they were now completely under McDonald's control. Having been gagged by his leader during the meeting, Topolski could not help but shovel a last sentiment back through the door: 'You arseholes, you've ruined the Boat Race,' he cried. His outburst seemed to signify his loss of control of 'his Boat Race'. Over the years, things had changed. His loss in 1986 and the onset of professional coaching that was set up for 1988 signified the end of 'his Boat Race'. This wasn't quite the Grand Finale he had planned for.

Silence filled the room for the few minutes after their departure. Everyone was horrified by McDonald's threats and the abusive manner that he had used to conduct the meeting. It was obvious that his threats had greatly disturbed many of the crew. 'Fortunately, Fish acted quickly and took control; he recognised that real fear that they felt about losing their Blues and not being allowed to row in the Boat Race,' said Clark. 'He quickly put things into perspective by recognising the importance of getting everyone to talk before McDonald's shock treatment took effect.' Gradually, as they talked, their fears subsided and were replaced by anger. They were angry that McDonald thought he had the right to treat them like that, and to lay down the law without first discussing the issue with them. They were disgusted at being treated like a bunch of nobodies, and they refused to believe that he could get away with it. 'He had no right to try and bully his way into the crew like that: his behaviour goes against everything that the Boat Race and a student boat club embody,' said Fish.

In the space of an hour, from having no contact with their President or Chief Coach, the selection disagreement had been escalated by McDonald into a full-blown war. McDonald was obviously prepared to sacrifice all his best oarsmen and the chance to preside over what would probably be the fastest Boat Race crew on record, and also to sacrifice the integrity of Oxford rowing by letting an inferior crew compete against Cambridge on Boat Race day, just so that he could row. This he had made perfectly clear in his speech. His only gain would be that he would have maintained his own authority and his own place in the crew. It seemed most bizarre to the crew that McDonald felt the need to act this way, forcing his authority upon them by laying down an ultimatum. His action was completely over the top and so out of character that the crew still believed that it was Topolski who was pulling the strings. After all, it did seem that this type of showdown was far more characteristic of Topolski's flamboyant fiery nature than it did of the quiet, sly McDonald. Of course, at this stage the oarsmen who sat in Vincent's had no idea of the immense network of advice which had led to the delivery of this 'cunning plan'. However, regardless of whoever was calling the shots, they had until midnight to respond to McDonald's ultimatum. McDonald's demands made a mockery of their intelligence, and they all quickly agreed that they wouldn't accept McDonald's request to ban Lyons, Clark and Fish from the Boat Race. Nobody, they agreed, would respond to the request to make a decision by midnight; instead, to try to salvage a sense of perspective and hopefully retrieve their chance of rowing in the Boat Race, they resolved to send a representative delegation of the whole squad to McDonald's house that evening to talk through the mess and come to some sort of amicable arrangement before he laid down any more ludicrous ultimatums.

Sensing that McDonald might not be very approachable, the delegation of Cadoux-Hudson, Hull, Penney, Stewart, Huntington and Gleeson asked Richard Yonge to go with them to talk with McDonald. Yonge is a good friend of McDonald and of Topolski, and previously had been President of the Boat Club. They hoped McDonald would be more amenable if they had a trusted arbitrator with them. Judging by the stony-faced greeting that Yonge received when McDonald opened the door, it was lucky that they took him along. Once inside, they hoped to appeal to McDonald's better nature and to get him to take back his ultimatum. His performance that afternoon had left them scared, scared for their Blues and scared that McDonald had really blown all hope of resolving the dispute. Each individual had his own motivation for wanting to sort things out. They were not by any means political giants; their primary motivation was to return the Boat Club to a status quo as quickly as possible. They were all shocked by the scare-mongering tactics McDonald had used in Vincent's, and hoped that in his own home, McDonald would feel more relaxed and able to talk things over.

Richard Hull pointed out that they had not come to apologise for challenging McDonald's selection decisions or to back down, but to apologise for the way they handled challenging him, and to explain why they wanted the selection to continue. 'We were prepared to admit that we should have been more considerate, we were sorry that McDonald had taken our meeting in Lyons's room so badly, it certainly wasn't meant to be confrontational, but it ended up that way,' Hull told me. They gave McDonald their sincere apologies, and then tried to negotiate. McDonald, however, was immediately defensive. 'Does this mean you want to row?' he asked, maintaining his steely exterior, obviously not prepared to talk. You can imagine the atmosphere in the room: McDonald, barriers up, refusing to hear what they had to say; Hull and Gleeson trying hard to find his sense of justice; Stewart pleading for McDonald to just listen to them for one moment; and Huntington and Penney authoritatively and educatedly trying to entice McDonald to communicate with them. None were successful. 'We all had the feeling that we were knocking our heads against a brick wall,' said Stewart. 'Despite everything that we said, McDonald remained adamant that he was right. The whole evening was just incomprehensible.'

The presence of his wife and children and of Richard Yonge helped to keep McDonald calm and to keep emotions locked away as much as was humanly possible, but even that didn't help in getting McDonald to discuss a solution. They tried every possible angle to find out how McDonald interpreted the dispute. He didn't make it easy for them, but they got the feeling that it was the McDonald versus Clark issue that bothered him most, and by dropping Lyons and Fish, he thought he had removed Clark's allies. Without their support, it seemed that McDonald had concluded that Clark wouldn't bother to fight on. He was right, Clark wouldn't have insisted that there should be more trials without the backing of the other members of the Boat Club. He had had enough, and was tired of all the trouble. Unlike McDonald, he wasn't the sort of person to stand up for his own ability without the support of those who he would be rowing with. McDonald was blind to the real issue, that Ward had been unjustly left out of the crew. It obviously hadn't crossed McDonald's mind that Ward was a part of the equation.

If it did nothing else, their visit that evening did make

McDonald see that excluding Lyons and Fish from the crew as well as Clark was not a good idea. I think he realised that, as they were not a part of the actual selection dispute, he would have difficulty justifying this action even to his most ardent supporters. However, he didn't mention his change of mind until somewhat later. Stewart telephoned McDonald from home later that evening; he had two suggestions which he hoped McDonald would consider. The suggestions were aimed at getting the crew, or rather a crew, back on the water. He felt that it was important to get communication going between the whole squad. He suggested that they should start rowing again with a crew that would include Lyons and Fish but leave Clark out, so that McDonald could row; McDonald seemed to open up, and agreed this was a good idea. Secondly, Stewart suggested that they should let Mike Spracklen decide who should be in the crew, McDonald or Clark. He picked Spracklen as an arbitrator because he knew that he would select with the best interests of the crew at heart, and because everybody trusted him. McDonald accepted this suggestion too, although he warned it would be difficult to get Mike to agree to make the decision because he had made it clear that he didn't want to be involved. The next morning there was a meeting in Tony Ward's room. Stewart passed on the result of his conversation with McDonald; they had at least survived the midnight deadline: a good sign, they thought.

It was now Friday, five days after Spracklen's first outing with the Oxford Blue Boat. Although his crew wasn't actually training, Mike went down to the Scout Camp every day in case they turned up for an outing. He realised that the situation was difficult, and wanted to be available to coach should a crew turn up. He felt that it would be helpful to morale if at least there was a coach on hand. This particular day, he found not a crew but Steve Royle and McDonald waiting for him at the Scout Camp. They had come to Marlow to ask Spracklen if he would select the crew, as Stewart had suggested to McDonald. They didn't, however, approach it in quite the manner he had meant them to. 'Tell them all to come back and row, you know they'll listen to you, the Boat Race is bigger than the both of us,' Steve Royle told Mike. It was a comment which would put their long friendship in jeopardy. Mike felt it was not for him to decide who should row in the crew, although, as he had said before to Clark and to McDonald, in his opinion Clark was the better oarsman. Spracklen repeated he didn't want to be involved. McDonald had expected this reply and had prepared an alternative to get Mike involved. If he wouldn't decide, 'would he go to a meeting of all the coaches where all the coaches could collectively decide who should be in the crew?' Mike eventually agreed to this, because he knew the oarsmen would trust his word if he said the selection panel had been fair.

McDonald's plan was crafty: Stewart and he had agreed to speak again should Mike refuse to make the selection decision himself. They had not agreed that he should organise a selection panel with coaches to make the decision. They were disheartened when they heard that McDonald had taken things into his own hands again, although McDonald did try to reassure them that he had acted in everyone's interest. They rang Mike to ask him what he thought they should do. 'Go along with the meeting: rationality will prevail,' Mike assured them, 'if all of the coaches get together and discuss this between themselves; trust me.' As they did trust him, they decided to take his advice and so agreed to abide by the collective decision of the coaches.

When Spracklen offered this advice he had no idea of the tactics which were to be employed at the meeting. He had agreed to attend an unbiased selection meeting to select the Blue Boat, but had not agreed to go to a meeting whose sole purpose was to ensure that McDonald would row in the crew and be allowed to continue as President unopposed.

11

Sunday, 25 January, 1987, was the date of the meeting of the chosen representatives and coaches of the OUBC. It was supposedly a meeting to decide who should be in the 1987 Blue Boat. There were eleven people present, including Topolski and McDonald; of the other nine, only two had recently been involved with the coaching, Spracklen and Royle. The remaining six had various associations with the club: Hugh Matheson, rowing correspondent for *The Independent* newspaper and Oxford Blue, due to coach the Blue Boat after Mike's stint; Mark Lees, professional coach of the University of London Boat Club, who had coached the previous year for a two-week period; Freddie Smallbone, who had coached the squad in the autumn; John Pilgrim-Morris, who had also coached, but again not since the autumn; Ronnie Howard, President of the University Boat Club at the time of the 1959 dispute, and Chairman of the President's Advisory Committee; and Dick Fishlock, an Oxford Blue who was appointed Chairman for the meeting. In all, quite an impressive line-up of past Oxford coaches and rowers. However, between them only the three, Topolski, Royle and Spracklen could claim to have coached or even studied closely the Oxford Blue Boat squad over the last six weeks. For the other coaches, their combined knowledge of the current squad was limited to coaching in the early autumn and to information given to them by Topolski, whom they had no reason to doubt. There was no-one at the meeting to represent the rowers who were claiming that selection was unfair and the management of the squad unjust.

Fishlock started business. As Chairman, he spoke at

length about the purpose of the meeting, and outlined that they had a sad and serious problem on their hands, which as a coaching team they were responsible to resolve. He wanted to make it clear that they were a team and that they should all agree to stand by the majority decision, whatever the outcome. 'They must,' he said, 'be loyal to this cabinet-like decision, and should undertake not to talk to anyone about the proceedings of the meeting or the individual preferences that each coach may have had.' In that way he proposed, as Chairman, that they would be able to solve the problems that McDonald and Topolski were facing. All the coaches agreed that they would, as he suggested, abide by a majority decision. Fishlock then went to some length to explain that as President, McDonald had total authority over his coaches and the selection decisions for the crew, and that, as coaches appointed to coach by McDonald, their loyalty should stand with him. Everyone listened, no-one spoke. Fishlock had a captive audience, but he still hadn't made it clear exactly what they were being asked to do. He had told them what their duties were as coaches 'employed' by the OUBC and its President, and made it very clear that the meeting was to put an end to a dispute.

'It was as if we were being told that whatever the question was, our vote should support the President, and that was our total role as coaches,' said Spracklen. He was the only one of the coaches to have spoken to the disputing oarsmen, and the only one who knew that the oarsmen had agreed that McDonald should hold this meeting to make a selection decision about the crew. The other coaches had been asked to come to the meeting 'to sort out the problems they were having in the Boat Club'; they had no other information available to them, only knowing what McDonald and Topolski had told them and information gleaned from a few press articles. Mark Lees, for example, told me that as a close friend of Topolski's he had had several conversations with him throughout the year about the problems he was having with the squad and with Clark in particular. Topolski had asked Lees's advice whether he thought he should get rid of Clark before Christmas; his advice was no: Clark was, in his opinion, a good oarsman worth having in the crew. He had coached Clark last year and appreciated he could be difficult to coach. 'He is a big talker, very sure of his own ability, and he needs to respect you and feel that you are worthy of his attention. And if he does, then you're OK,' Lees told me. 'It was fairly common knowledge that he could be difficult to coach, and I convinced Topolski to bear with him.' When Topolski rang to ask him to attend a meeting, he said to Lees that it was about Clark and his American friends. Lees said he asked for no more information as he felt in the know. John Pilgrim-Morris and Freddie Smallbone also felt in the know: they, too, apparently understood how difficult Clark could be. Ronnie Howard knew from McDonald that Clark was the cause of the trouble, and so did Matheson.

However, the truth was somewhat different, as none of them understood the problem at all; they knew only a one-sided story. Even Royle, who had been more closely involved than the rest of the panel, didn't really understand how final the decision they were to make would be; he thought they were there to put the oarsmen into an 'A' and 'B' squad. He told me adamantly that 'there were to be further selection trials, that the squad had only to be split up into two groups. This stage of the proceedings was just the start, the two crews were an experiment'. He was in no doubt that the meeting was not to decide the Blue Boat composition, but to decide two squads; he was mistaken. In my opinion, these coaches were seriously misinformed and they behaved unprofessionally in allowing the meeting to continue without first considering why there was such a big problem. The coaches seem to have blindly accepted that they were employed by the President and held by 'contract of the Boat Club Constitution to support the President', regardless of the situation. If that were the case, there would have been no point in holding such a meeting. As it was, it is straightforward enough to conclude that they were not all in agreement on the exact purpose of the meeting, thus making any decisions taken seem like false representation of their collective opinion.

The meeting had been going for quite a while by the time Topolski was asked to outline the selection issue between McDonald and Clark. Everything prior to that had covered the issue of the coaches' loyalty to the President, the importance of confidentiality, and the undisputed qualifications of Topolski as a coach. When Topolski was finally asked to outline the selection issues, he presented a synopsis of the individual performance of Clark and McDonald in the gym, on the ergometer and out on the water. He outlined a winter of discontent in which Clark had been the main cause of many arguments over training whilst not completing it himself. He produced the results of ergo tests, sculling races and gym tests in which Clark scored badly or did not even feature, but in which McDonald excelled. There was no mention of the rib injury with which he had started the year. The ergometer scores they were given were the ones scored when he was jet-lagged after returning from the USA after Christmas. His much-improved performance over the last six weeks was not even mentioned. Nor did Topolski bother to reiterate that he was an international oarsman who had clearly demonstrated his skills at a number of international events, and there was no mention that the initial cause of the dispute had been because Clark was put in the crew on bowside instead of Ward. He summarised the seat racing in which Clark had beaten McDonald on strokeside and then been slaughtered on bowside by Cadoux-Hudson, emphasising that Clark was fit without drawing attention to the fact that he was a better oarsman then McDonald. Instead, he used this to support his argument that the bowside race demonstrated Clark was performing well on both sides of the boat. Topolski also made little of the Seat Race result by casting doubts over the fairness of the race. Nor was it mentioned that the majority of the Oxford squad considered the fastest eight men to be Huntington, Penney, Cadoux-Hudson, Hull, Lyons, Ward, Clark and Stewart; the only issue they discussed thoroughly was Clark versus McDonald. Topolski also took great pains to outline how thorough McDonald had been in his winter training, although that wasn't really in question.

The Seat Races at Henley were discussed at length because it seemed to the coaches to be a hole in Topolski's defence; the majority of the individuals present did at least want to understand precisely what had happened and why it had become so controversial. McDonald joined in to help

Topolski explain. He told them how he felt Penney had cheated by not pulling in the first race and then raising the rates in the second to give Clark an unfair advantage. However, the racing McDonald outlined and the cheating he accused Penney of was, of course, nothing more than pure supposition. However, after a long and heated debate, the race, as evidence, was cast aside. The only concrete thing about the race was that Clark's crew crossed the line first, two-thirds of a length ahead of McDonald's. Endless discussion and confusion, with Topolski and McDonald describing and defending the training and selection, seemed to highlight two salient factors: Clark was obviously a problem for the coaches, and McDonald had trained hard and demonstrated his fitness as well as making it clear he was not a problem for the coaches. Clark began to come off worse whilst the issue surrounding the rest of the squad dissolved into the background. They were right that McDonald had trained hard and that until after Christmas Clark hadn't. But that wasn't the root of the problem. They didn't question what else was involved, nor whether hard training automatically gives a man the right to a place in the crew. Topolski and McDonald had clearly made up their minds that they wanted to get rid of Clark, and this meeting was a mere formality to do just that.

Each coach had his own wish to see the dispute settled, and each suffered his own torment about whether the evidence they saw before them was clear enough for them to make a fair selection decision. Jeff Jacobs, the Isis coach, made a point which demonstrated their dilemma. Jacobs said that Clark was the best man for the job, 'if the coaches could handle his psychology'; nodding heads showed that they all agreed. When asked, every single coach said that they could personally handle Clark's psychology if he were in a crew they were coaching: from this, you would have thought that they all agreed that Clark was the best oarsman for the job. But still they debated the relative performances and looked for other ways to come to a decision. Mark Lees suggested that trials should be carried out in Pairs, and Spracklen suggested that an ergometer test would be better; as he of course knew that there was no one suitable for McDonald to row with. Fishlock, Topolski and McDonald remained adamant that a selection decision should be made that evening before they ended the meeting; they felt that more selection trials would only give strength to the 'rebellion'. How wrong they were. Further selection by a panel of agreed coaches was what the crew asked for, and at least one of the coaches present (Steven Royle) thought that selection would still continue regardless of the outcome of the meeting. Fish later said, in an article in *The Times* (7 February, 1987), 'If McDonald is in fact better than Clark, he should not have any difficulty proving it to the rest of the squad'; however, the feeling remained that more trials would be unfair because there would be too much hard feeling to make all the oarsmen pull their weight. The only reason for selection not to continue was because the chief coach and the President didn't want it to.

During the meeting, Spracklen had said very little. He was there only because McDonald, Royle and the crew had been so insistent upon his attendance. When he did speak it was in order to set a different perspective upon the extremely single-minded direction which the meeting seemed to have taken on, but his vague attempts to look at things from the oarsmen's point of view were snubbed. He wasn't acting as their spokesman because he had said he would not. As a well-respected coach world-wide, his words held a lot of credibility. If he had disagreed with the decisions made at the meeting, then others would doubt the integrity of those decisions. Yet he wasn't really the perfect spokesman for the crew, because his dislike of politics and meetings was registered by a strong silence, whilst the other coaches debated the oarsmen's ability and Clark's worthiness. It was not in his style to try to force his arguments upon others, and his only interjections were to try to steer the subject back to the difference between Clark and McDonald as the conversation kept drifting back to Clark's bad behaviour and the hard training which McDonald had put in all winter. He wanted them to discuss rowing ability, not worthiness. 'Clark,' he pointed out, 'is an international standard oarsman, whilst McDonald is a club standard oarsman; there is no comparison.' Mark Lees supported Clark as the better oarsman, as did Jacobs. Lees had even gone as far as to tell Topolski before he arrived at the meeting that, in his opinion, Clark was better than McDonald. 'McDonald,' he said, 'is a stiff and unwieldy oarsman.' Lees abstained from the final vote, however, in respecting Topolski's decision, because he had agreed to stand by a majority decision at the beginning of the meeting, and because he said that despite voting on who was the better oarsman, the issue wasn't really about the difference in their rowing ability. 'As one of the President's coaches you must stand by his decision; he should be in complete control. Anyway, they didn't really need Clark, they had a lot of talent without him. In retrospect I believe he should have been sacked from the squad before,' Lees told me emphatically.

Fishlock finally called for a vote. 'It seems to me to be a straight case between Clark and McDonald,' he announced. He then went around the room individually and asked each coach for their decision. He started with John Pilgrim-Morris, an Establishment man who stood by McDonald. Jacobs, too, despite his earlier statement, voted for McDonald. Lees came half-way through the count; 'I find it hard to vote on this issue because I have not coached Clark recently,' he abstained. Everyone else stood by McDonald except Spracklen, who voted for Clark. The final vote was seven for the President, one abstension and one against. Had the vote been taken by only those three coaches who had coached in the last six weeks, Spracklen, Royle and Topolski, the vote would be one for Clark and two against, but Royle's vote couldn't possibly count considering that he was voting not to sack Clark completely, but to form an 'A' and 'B' squad. The truth was that none of the coaches in that room, except Topolski and Spracklen, were qualified to vote on who was the best oarsman, and none of them realised the finality of their vote. In reality, the motion passed was not about who was the better oarsman, but whether the coaches supported the Establishment and so allowed the President to select and manage his crews as he saw fit. The importance of the President's authority had been impressed upon them throughout. There is little doubt that this was the true motion upon which they took a vote.

The meeting and vote made it impossible for the oarsmen to have any further influence over the formation of their Boat Race crew. It moved from being a domestic dispute between oarsmen and coaches as soon as the meeting was publicly announced, and after McDonald's press release it became an issue for the public to debate. Daily articles in the national press told how the Oxford University Boat Club President was under seige by five American rebel oarsmen who were about to take charge of the Boat Club and cast aside its long-entrusted coaches so that Clark, the only American not selected and a good friend of the other Americans, could row. The Americans were attacked in a vicious and personal way for daring to challenge the running or the coaches of our great British institution, the Boat Race.

The first instalment of the '1987 Boat Race Mutiny' story was told by Geoffrey Page and was published in the *Daily Telegraph* on the Friday before the Leander meeting, Friday 21 January. Page's headline read, 'Oxford Crew Rift Brings Ultimatum', and in the article he deftly classified an American-led rebellion. From where his information came, Page does not state; however, the very nature of its content does not point to an oarsman as the source. The press never really got the story right, although particular journalists, American and British, did get some of the details right toward the end of the dispute. However, once the story came out it seemed to keep going on its own, fuelled by public interest and press sensationalism that portrayed the Americans as the guys trying to overturn a great British tradition. The American-led rebellion was a great story, and once it gathered momentum became difficult to refute. The press of course wouldn't have known the full story, for like the coaches at the meeting at the Leander Club, they were completely unaware of the other side of the coin: no-one ever spoke to the oarsmen until they already had well-formed questions to ask them about the stories that were already taken as read. There were numerous lines of attack the press could have taken; it is just a pity for the crew that they never chose to debate whether being President of the Boat Club should give you the right to row in the Boat Race, and to cast aside oarsmen of greater skill and potential than yourself. They could, too, have chosen to unravel the mysteries of sports selection, but instead chose to concoct a typically British story of American interference and international misunderstanding of 'the way things are done over here'. The absurdity of it all is that most of us who are proud to be British would hastily deny that our sporting teams should be made up of those who supposedly deserve the honour, not those who are the best!

Obviously hopeful of an early end to the dispute, McDonald personally contacted Jim Railton of *The Times* and Chris Dodd of *The Guardian* and asked them to come along to Leander Club; he said after the meeting that he would issue a formal statement outlining the proceedings of the meeting. Neither of them actually sat in on the meeting but both waited patiently in the bar for McDonald's promised statement. On Monday 26 January, 1987, Jim Railton wrote in *The Times*, 'Oxford University yesterday attempted to quell their Boat Race Mutiny by sacking Christopher Clark, one of the five Americans in their squad. After a crisis meeting. . . lasting almost five hours, the President, Donald McDonald, appeared to have regained control. . . Afterwards, McDonald issued the following statement: I have made it clear that I have invited my team of coaches, under the leadership of Daniel Topolski, to select the crew; this would not be conditional on the President being in the crew or even party to the selection. This meeting fully endorsed the policy. . . The coaches discussed the relative merits of those under selection, and came to the conclusion that, since Chris Clark had failed to honour the demands made of him in training on a number of occasions, he will not be invited to continue.'

Dodd's article in *The Guardian* wasn't much different and both articles implied, as McDonald had told them in his statement, that the meeting was a selection meeting in which the American oarsman, Chris Clark, had been deselected from the Boat Race squad because he was a troublemaker and a dishonourable sportsman. With such an introduction to the dispute the public can be excused for supporting McDonald and thinking that Clark had finally got what he deserved.

12

At 1 pm on the day after the Leander meeting, Huntington and Lyons walked to Oriel Square to meet McDonald to tell him that none of the crew were happy with the decision made, and that they would not be going to Marlow for an outing. They told him that they wanted a meeting with the coaches so that they could speak to them face to face. They found it odd that none of the coaches were prepared to state their opinions publicly, and they didn't trust McDonald's explanation of how the meeting had gone. It just didn't seem quite right to them, and they guessed that he had personally instigated their silence. That they had not thought of approaching the coaches before the meeting demonstrated their faith in McDonald's honesty and clearly showed the different approach the two sides had when it came to trying to solve differences of opinion. On the one hand, McDonald and his old Blues trusted no-one and left nothing to chance, whereas the oarsmen believed implicitly that their requests were reasonable and would be dealt with justly. McDonald had thought out every move he made; winning this dispute was merely a tactical problem to him. He had been quick to ascertain support from the coaching team before the crew had a chance to speak to them, and he made sure that once they had all given their support it was announced publicly in the press as a 'unanimous decision' to drop Clark from the squad.

The reports had been printed in the papers that morning. Now that he had their support, he was at liberty to let the crew talk to them. I think that he hoped that if the coaches showed their support for him, the 'mutineers' would have to shut up and row, or else stand down from the crew; either way the dispute would be over. Had the crew realised the extent to which the President was prepared to go, and realised the power that he had at his fingertips, they might well have taken steps to fight for their own rights in an equally well-organised and determined manner. So far, McDonald had been one step ahead of them all the time. Had they spent some time with the coaches before the meeting at Leander and before McDonald's version of the dispute had been firmly planted in their minds, and before the whole dispute had become public, they might well have overcome the President and settled the dispute in a more satisfactory manner. As it was, they were clearly fighting a losing battle. McDonald now had his story firmly entrenched in his coaches' minds.

McDonald called a meeting to take place that evening in St Giles House, St John's College, where he had asked the majority of coaches who had been at the meeting in Leander. Mark Lees, Freddie Smallbone and Hugh Matheson were absent. But in addition, Dr Michael Barry, the Boat Club Treasurer, who hadn't been to the previous meeting, had been invited. Spracklen again had to be persuaded to attend the meeting; after Sunday's get-together he was less than happy about becoming further involved. From the crew, Stewart, Clark, Huntington, Penney, Hull, Lyons, Fish and Ward went along to put forward their side of the argument. However, they were somewhat dismayed when they arrived at St Giles. By the time they got there McDonald had already seated the coaches formally around a big U-shaped table. Fishlock, as Chairman, sat in the middle with McDonald, Topolski and Dr Barry on his right, and Spracklen, Royle and Pilgrim-Morris on his left. This left room for the oarsmen on the other side of the table: the seating arrangements clearly were part of the power-psychology play which was being used to ensure that the coaches felt strength in their togetherness. The table presented a physical barrier positioned to protect the coaches from any real contact with the crew. A far cry from the informal meeting which the crew had requested, where they had hoped that they would be able to get all concerned to sit down and discuss in a civilised fashion how best to resolve this dispute. They wanted to remove the pomp and ceremony which was shutting out reason and rationality. But McDonald had once again surpassed himself, never for a moment allowing anyone to catch him off his guard. The maintenance of such a formal atmosphere constantly reaffirmed the severity of the issues at stake. The only shortfall of this approach was that the coaches were so much on their guard that they expected a direct confrontation with a bunch of rebellious, arrogant 'loud-mouthed Yanks'. But this wasn't the impression they received. The three Britons and five American oarsmen who faced them across the table were unanimous in their appeal for reason and fairness and, for a moment, McDonald stood alone. As the crew talked and explained their predicament rationality almost broke through the formal facade.

McDonald started the meeting by reminding everybody that at the Leander meeting the coaches' decision had been unanimously in favour of dropping Christopher Clark from the Boat Race squad. Spracklen immediately intervened and reiterated that the vote wasn't unanimous, that he had voted against the majority decision. The boys were grateful for Spracklen's intervention, 'grateful for Mike being Mike', said Fish. 'It gave them all the boost they needed to get started on what looked like being a thankless task.' McDonald's speech over, the floor was open for the first crew member to speak. Gavin started by explaining the situation as they, the crew, saw it. He said he was embarrassed by the way that the Americans were being treated because it was he who had started the dispute because 'a personal friend of his', Tony Ward, was left out of the crew to let in 'an inferior oarsman' (by that he meant McDonald). 'The Americans,' he said, 'joined us, and now one of them was being made a scapegoat for their action.' He then went on to outline how they could not appreciate how the arguments which had now banished Clark from the Boat Race, ie his lack of training, bad behaviour and psychology, could possibly be vindicated, since they had obviously not been considered a problem when Clark was selected to row on bowside the day after the Seat Races at Henley. He admitted that there had been complaints about Clark before Christmas, but that since the post-Christmas training camp there had been none. Clark had completed the training along with the rest of them, and he had more than proven his worth. 'Clark was selected to row on one day, and then, using the opposite arguments he was dropped the next.' No man can have such a change in worthiness in one day, particularly not on a day when there were no trials taking place!

The coaches listened intently. Stewart was an oarsman who had been rowing for Oxford for many years, and a lot of those coaches knew him well. He is a respected man and the arguments he offered made sense. He told them that they considered this a matter of grave importance: they were 'concerned that the fastest crew had not been selected. . . all we want is some fair testing and some more trials in the interest of finding the fastest crew.' Following his speech, the conversation began to flow freely across the table. This was more the sort of rational communication you would expect to witness between friends and respected professionals. Relieved to be airing their opinions, they were all able to discuss the problems that were troubling them. The freedom of speech meant that at last both sides could ask whatever questions they felt necessary. 'Even Topolski,' said Huntington, 'was showing the reason that I knew he was capable of.' They were no longer locked in a heartless battle of power, but were actually discussing their disagreements in the way that Spracklen had suggested to the crew that the coaches would. The interchange went on for a couple of hours, the coaches interested in what the crew had to say, and in the questions and answers that were passing to and fro across the table. At one point, Fish even went as far as to ask McDonald if he wanted the fastest crew; his reply was that he did but his floundering reaction showed that McDonald was in trouble; they felt they were reaching his conscience.

After the Boat Race, McDonald described that meeting at St Giles to journalist and ex-Olympic American oarsman Steve Kiesling as 'the blackest day of my life'. It was the only point in the dispute when he felt completely isolated in his determination to settle the dispute his way.

Having spent several hours debating the issues at stake, Fishlock moved to close the meeting. He asked the oarsmen to leave them to discuss the issue alone; he would let them know their decision shortly, he said, giving them a reassuring wink and passing comment as they left. 'We're big men here, the Boat Race is at stake. We have to make some kind of compromise.' The crew were satisfied that they had had their chance to speak, and left feeling that at last things were going to be sensibly sorted out. News reporters stood waiting outside for news of any decisions. They told them that no decision had yet been made, but 'it had been a productive meeting'. They were right, it had been a productive meeting, but as they left St Giles House, reason and rationality left with them. They had left a decidedly different atmosphere from the unpleasant one which had greeted them, and Fishlock assumed that McDonald too would be feeling slightly different after the talks. McDonald, however, felt no differently, except feeling a little worried that the coaches had been side-tracked and might reverse yesterday's decision. 'He was furious,' said Spracklen, and was once again calling the shots as he informed them all that what they had heard was nothing but an act. He called the Americans 'hard-nosed careerists' who thought they could run the Boat Race. 'Nothing has changed: if you were right yesterday then your decision is still right today.' McDonald challenged their sense of authority, 'stand with me or watch out' seemed to be his threat. At this point, sensing Spracklen's anger at the change of tack, Fishlock turned his back upon him and Royle and began a private consultation between himself, McDonald and Topolski. They were once again discussing leaving Clark out but this time they were facing up to the fact that they either had to pick Clark or accept that the rest of the crew would stand down and not row. McDonald was demanding that they 'shouldn't stand down. . . that they mustn't give in. . . that they shouldn't be bullied into doing anything for Clark. . .'

'It was outrageous,' said Mike. 'They weren't discussing the right thing to do, they were just discussing their warfare tactics; it was pure victimization of Chris Clark.' Spracklen was seething. To get attention, he stood up. The Chairman still had his back to him and was engrossed in a private conversation which, with Mike on his immediate left, I'm sure he was embarrassed about. Fishlock obviously didn't believe this was the right way to solve this problem, but he wasn't prepared to, or didn't think he had the power to challenge the President. Spracklen did.

Once he had their attention, Mike quietly said he would not be a party to this victimization, and that he was leaving. Attempts to calm Spracklen, and a request from Topolski for him to stay, put Mike back in his seat as once again they opened up discussion about what they should do. There is no doubt about the disgust Mike showed and felt about the whole proceedings. His refusal to change his mind and say that McDonald was a better oarsman than Clark, so that the coaches could stand united and support the President, left a difficult gap in their argument. In this situation, Clark could hardly have been said to have been dropped because he didn't deserve a place, regardless of the number of coaches whose support lay with the President. One of the most respected coaches in the world decided to challenge that decision, and therefore you are left with the feeling that all was not well. Spracklen had absolutely nothing to gain from supporting Clark and, more importantly, he had nothing to lose by supporting him either; he is not an Oxford man and his decision was purely performance-based.

The decision they finally reached that night did not even pose as a majority decision. In exasperation, Fishlock gave in to McDonald. 'We cannot make the decision for you,' he said. 'We are only to advise you as President; the final decision is yours.' At last given free rein, McDonald chose to stand by himself: Clark was out. The crew were recalled and told the news. Their disappointment and everybody else's embarrassment filled the air, because they knew this was not how to solve the crisis. The only person who didn't mind the hurt and resentment that the oarsmen showed was McDonald. Not even Topolski can claim to be sure of his President's decision at this point. In retrospect that meeting represented a frail point in McDonald's reign; his only saving grace was his own determination and the support that he had been shown up until then. Royle voiced the thoughts of the majority, 'as part of his coaching team you should always support the President, even if you don't always agree,' he said. It is difficult to judge whether the coaching team were right in supporting the President's decision. Theoretically, they had no power to dispute it. As Boat Club President, his Constitution gave him the power to select any crew and any coach to produce it that he wanted to. The only rein upon his power was the faith that the University and his fellow students bestowed upon him to choose the fastest crew to represent Oxford.

Having relinquished his power by asking the coaches to make a selection decision for him, the coaches had agreed, at the President's request, to compromise his power and make a decision for him. Two important points come to light from this. Firstly, McDonald asked them to make a decision for him, thereby admitting that his own direct involvement made him incapable of making an unbiased decision. Secondly it was the coaches' duty to do so by taking into account both sides of the dispute, which at the meeting at Leander they clearly did not. It is my opinion that, having agreed to adjudicate, they should have fulfilled their obligations as an arbitration panel. By returning the decision-making to McDonald, they did not. McDonald was certainly aware that their word would be law, regardless of his written power. He would almost certainly have had trouble with the Press, the public, the University and the oarsmen if he had continued without further trials and if they had chosen to reopen selection. When Fishlock renounced their involvement by handing the decision back to McDonald he made it easy for McDonald to justify whatever decision he chose, and, given this opportunity, he took it. He took back his power and dropped Clark even with the knowledge that the crew might refuse to row if he did. McDonald later told reporter Steve Kiesling that at 'that point he hated Fishlock and Topolski for not supporting him'; he wanted their support but made it plain that he would do without them if he had to. On hearing the decision, the crew refused to row. They could not believe what had happened between them leaving the room and the decision being announced. Refusing to row was their only possible means of showing how serious they thought the issue was.

With no crew to row with, McDonald knew he would

have to make the next move and it was his wife Ruth who came up with the next suggestion. She suggested that to get the crew rowing again, McDonald would have to sacrifice his own place in the crew, but only on the condition that Clark didn't row either. Paul Gleeson could row in his place. Ruth obviously realised that her husband's pride would never let him stand down if Clark still rowed. If neither of them rowed, Ruth obviously thought that her husband would be vindicated because he would still be President and could accept the glory of being a winning President. It was a true compromise, a chance for both sides to save face, but not really in the spirit of the Boat Race, which is not based upon compromise.

The offer was sent via Pelham, who was still in the fortunate position of talking to both sides. McDonald was quoted in *The Times* as saying that the offer was made 'because it might allow people to come together'. Topolski later suggested that if they didn't accept the suggestion then obviously their motives were only to have McDonald out and Clark in, and not, as they were stating, that they wanted fair selection and the fastet possible crew. But I think his argument had tinges of false logic. To accept this offer would mean losing the integrity which they had stood by so far. They said they wanted fair selection and the fastest possible crew: by accepting this offer they were merely labelling the dispute as a personal one. In fact, upon Clark's instruction they did try to accept his offer, but not until Wednesday, the day after the offer was sent out. McDonald sent back a message saying the offer had a deadline of Tuesday midnight, which they had missed.

By this stage, Clark, like many others, was pretty fed up with the whole affair. The constant press attention had sent him back to the safety of his studies where at least he could be confident his efforts would not be wasted. He was in the awkward position of knowing that he wasn't directly the cause of the dispute, but he also knew that if he wasn't there, the arguments would come to an end.

Clark, however, was not in control. The crew would not allow him to stand aside. By the time he received McDonald's offer to stand down he just wanted to see the mess cleared up: 'not rowing in the Boat Race seemed a small price to pay for peace and sanity, and to get the others back on the water,' he said. Understandably, the battle had become more of a personal one for him, more so than for the rest of the crew. He was unsure who deserved his hate the most, Topolski or McDonald; McDonald was calling the shots but Topolski seemed to be the one responsible for ruining the Boat Race, his rowing career and his integrity.

When McDonald offered to stand down, Clark was the one who persuaded the others to accept the offer. Strangely, no-one had bothered to ask Gleeson what he felt about it. He heard that he was to take the President's position in the crew on the radio. I suppose McDonald assumed that he would be glad of the chance of a Blue. As it turned out, he wasn't happy, he was rather annoyed by the lack of courtesy the President showed him, and didn't particularly want a Blue he hadn't earned. His feelings were demonstrable of the depth of disgust that now ran through the squad. All the crew members were being used as pawns in somebody else's game. Gleeson didn't get a chance to air his views on the matter because nobody even had the courtesy to ask him, although the rapid withdrawal of the offer made it irrelevant anyway. McDonald's wife's solution obviously didn't really fit. I have sympathy for him, it would have been a frustrating solution for both men; perhaps even more so for McDonald because he stood to gain nothing. He wouldn't really have had the glory of being a President who stood down to make way for a better man, but rather he would have been a President forced down. When he withdrew this offer he withdrew any chance of a compromise. He was going to row, with or without his present squad. He just needed another crew to race with him, so that he could offer another ultimatum to the rebels.

The crew he found was Isis, his second crew. They had been training throughout the dispute at Marlow under the direction of Olympic oarsman Steven Redgrave, and although many of them were in close contact with their friends in the Blue Boat squad, for the most part they had tried to continue their training. McDonald went to Marlow on Wednesday afternoon to speak directly to the Isis boys. He had a fairly icy reception. He didn't really carry much weight in the squad anymore. However, they did agree to listen to what he had to say. Then, left in consultation with their coaches, they made the decision to accept his offer and stand as the Blue Boat should they be asked. This allowed McDonald to issue yet another deadline. With the knowledge that he had a crew to race with he gave the rebels until Sunday night to agree to row. Otherwise, he said, he would employ Isis as the Blue Boat and this time he meant business.

Had Isis not agreed to act as the Blue Boat then he would have had to look elsewhere. But he even went as far as to say that he would row with the fastest combination of College oarsmen he could find. And I doubt that he would have had much trouble finding seven people who wanted a Blue they would otherwise have no chance of earning. Whether Isis should have been judged harshly for their decision I'm not sure. Their advisers were certainly unbiased: Redgrave was vaguely aware of the dispute, but said he had given up trying to follow what was going on as 'it was obvious that it was a private argument which the press had failed to interpret correctly'. In offering his advice to the crew he said he considered only their best interests. He couldn't and didn't think it necessary for them to make a value judgement on the dispute in order to make a decision about whether to row as the Blue Boat. He advised them to take advantage of the opportunity: for many it might be the only opportunity they would get to earn a full Blue. 'Sport can be a very selfish thing, everybody is out for themselves,' Redgrave suggested to them. 'Nobody will remember who was right or wrong, they will just remember who won the race and how good or bad the crews were. You would be mad not to take the chance.'

The crew decided that they would take their chance and if asked to row as the Blue Boat, they would. The only condition they gave to McDonald about this offer was that the crew which was to row was to be sorted out by the following Sunday. They could 'foresee an unsettling struggle right up to the race on 28 March as the dissidents returned one by one and displaced them', Matheson reported in *The Independent* on 29 January. They weren't prepared to accept that.

13

'They all had very strong personalities and believed vehemently in what they were fighting for,' Royle told me, referring to the American contingent. He was right on both counts. Their strong personalities were very prominent during the whole dispute, so much so that they tended to overshadow the equally strong, although not so outspoken, British contingent. They too had strong personalities, and believed that the Boat Club was being badly run, and that the oarsmen were being unfairly treated. However, their part in the dispute was made less public than the part that their American counterparts played, purely because the Press were determined to play on the American angle.

In reality, in the first week it was the tireless efforts of the Brits to fight for justice which gave the Americans the courage to stand their ground. Hull and Stewart in particular spent a lot of time with Lyons and Fish, trying to keep pace with the President's rapid moves and acting as spokesmen for the whole crew. Clark was not central to any decision-making until the dispute reached deadlock, when he finally accepted that he was not going to be able to row whilst McDonald was still President and Topolski still Chief Coach. As for Huntington and Penney, they were not as motivated to stand their ground in the same way that Lyons and Fish were until after the meeting at St. Giles. Until then, they had taken a back seat in the proceedings and hoped that rationality would prevail before too much harm was done. They were optimistic that the differences would be sorted out amicably. However, after the meeting at St. Giles, their optimism was dashed. They rapidly learnt that they were dealing with Establishment fanatics, and that their emotion and feeling to preserve that Establishment was far more important than anything else. Pointing out the truth to these fanatics was not regarded with any favour! It was not until the full horror of the deception and manipulative tactics that McDonald was prepared to use, that Penney and Huntington gave themselves wholeheartedly to the cause, determined that McDonald should not be allowed to get away with such deception. 'Warfare is built on deception,' Socrates said, and here was a prime example. The idea that McDonald was prepared to let the coaches decide what should happen was pure deception: his final decision at the St. Giles meeting demonstrated that. Once they recognised the deception, their determination to fight back was refuelled. It was this fire and determination which the Press picked up in their reports of the dispute. It obviously matched perfectly with the first information they received on the dispute of fiery, outspoken Americans, 'the sort of Americans Oxford can do without' (Simon Barnes, 10 February, *The Times*). There was then no need to include the Britons in their reports. In fact, it made a better story to report the British guys as meek, misguided followers. The Americans, too, had expertise on their side. Being World and Olympic medallists gave them credibility and their voices recognition, and made them seem more in the forefront than the likes of Gavin Stewart, Tony Ward and Richard Hull, whose notable rowing achievements were not as impressive: Ward was the only ex-junior International, and none of them were current Internationals. The American oarsmen were set up as the 'leaders' of the 'rebel camp', and once that label had been given, courtesy of the Press, they found considerable difficulty in shaking it off.

They made a start by trying to make contact with the journalists concerned. By the middle of the second week, the journalists had still not made any contact with the oarsmen, despite the reports which had appeared in the major papers daily since the release of the very first report of problems as Oxford, written by Geoffrey Page for *The Daily Telegraph* on Friday, 21 January, before the meeting at Leander Club, followed by daily reports in *The Guardian, The Times* and, spuriously, by *The Independent, The Daily Express* and *The Mail.* The Americans' attempts to refute the stories released daily in the papers served to entangle them further in the arguments and confuse the issue (which the journalists were doing a good job of confusing, anyway).

The dispute was complicated with tension and high emotion by the time the first story was printed. The emotions, coupled with the confusion between the two sides about who had said what and when, made it very difficult for the Press to get to grips with what was going on. Page's first report in *The Daily Telegraph* said the problem was 'a competition between McDonald and Clark for the number two seat in this year's crew' (Friday, 21 January), a problem caused, said Railton, by 'an embarrassment of riches, with a strong American influence and desperate challenges for marginal seats. . . it appears that members within the squad feel they can pick the crew themselves' (*The Times,* 22 January).

The regular rowing correspondents, Dodd, Page and Railton, were ever-hopeful of the President 'regaining control' even in the early stages. We heard from both Railton of *The Times* and Dodd of *The Guardian* that a meeting of all the coaches under Topolski was organised by the President to 'select the crew'. Dodd and Railton assured us that that meeting endorsed the policy that Clark would be dropped because he had 'failed to honour his training commitments'. But, said Railton, with no reference to the whole crew, just to the Americans, 'It remains to be seen how the talented American contingent react to the President's statement. . . I cannot see the Oxford Establishment giving way' (*The Times,* 26 January).

Dodd got a little closer to the truth on Tuesday, 27 January, when he suggested that 'When the Californian was left out of the trial boat and the quiet Scot put in, there were accusations that Clark's tests had been better and that justice was not being seen to be done. . .'

Anyone reading Matheson's first attempt at informing his readership of the problems would have found justification for Clark being left out. On the front page of *The*

Independent, Matheson outlined the two sides to the dispute: 'On the one side, representing the Establishment, are the President of the Oxford University Boat Club, Donald McDonald, and his Chief Coach, Dan Topolski. On the other is a large group of key oarsmen, notably their five talented Americans who have said that if Clark goes, then so do they.' At least Matheson had the decency to include Clark as one of the talented oarsmen, although the rest of his article leaves you wondering how he can possibly be talented: indeed whether any of them deserve to be at the University let alone take part in the Boat Race. 'The Americans are mostly on one-year post-graduate diploma of Social Science courses, using Oxford as an enjoyable break from yuppie careers,' said Matheson mischievously (*The Independent*, 27 January). Matheson went on to reiterate that, despite finding the Americans' behaviour not really what should be expected, 'It is probable that the dissatisfaction within the crew goes wider than the issue of Clark, and covers the whole selection procedure. This is not unusual,' he said, 'but has never been as publicly acrimonious before.'

Remember, Matheson was at the Leander meeting and was due to be coaching the crew in the next week, yet his first report for *The Independent* demonstrates that, even three days after the meeting, he was unable to explain what the real problem was; he publicly announced that he wasn't even sure if the arguments involved more than Clark, evidence that the decision of the meeting should not have been carried, because not all of the coaches at the meeting fully understood the implications of the problem.

By the 27th, Railton too got clued into the idea of discontent amongst the whole squad, and not just between McDonald and Clark. He reported, 'It appears that the Americans are leading, but there are other members of the squad who are not happy with the selection. The great worry is that the majority of the crew will pull out' (*The Times*, 27 January). At least he acknowledged the seriousness of their arguments by indicating that there must have been a lot of unhappy people if the 'majority' were thinking of pulling out. Thankfully, Matheson's report the following day seemed a little more informed and cleared up a few misconceptions: 'Originally, the discontent arose when Ward, 19 of Oriel College was displaced at number three by Clark. . . The crew protested that Ward would do better in his specialised position, and that Clark should go back on to strokeside and replace the President himself' (*The Independent,* 28 January). Matheson was clearly approaching the truth, although it was a great pity that the rest of his article sought to undermine Clark personally, and suggested that the coaches were right to drop Clark in favour of McDonald because: 'Clark had failed to honour training agreements, and because the past week he had tried to hijack the crew by persuading some others not to row except in a crew of their own selection.'

In fact it was the crew who told Clark that they wouldn't row until the selection disagreements were sorted out, and not Clark who was leading the way, and we also know that the dispute was not started by outraged Americans at all, but by the Britons, particularly Stewart, who felt loyalty to his crewmates and was disgusted by the underhand selection methods, which seemed to be misleading and inaccurate. The Britons asked for support from the rest of the potential 'A' squad, including the Americans, in refusing to see Ward left out of the crew because he had already demonstrated his skill over Clark on bowside. Clark became the centre of attention on the following day when, for no apparent reason, he went from being good enough to be in the 'A' squad to being dropped from the Boat Race team altogether.

The headlines on Wednesday, 28 January, were full of the President's offer to stand down from his place in the Blue Boat in an attempt to 'quell the mutiny over selection methods' (*The Independent,* 28 January). 'But the terms of his conditional offer are designed to prevent the return of American oarsman Chris Clark' (*The Guardian,* 28 January).

Railton in *The Times* was one step ahead of his fellow journalists when he said that the offer was 'snubbed by the Boat Race crew who had the support of one of Britain's leading coaches, Mike Spracklen' (*The Times,* 28 January).

The crew did indeed quote the support of Spracklen, but at that point assured me that they did not even know of McDonald's actual offer officially; they had only heard it from journalists, hardly, they felt, a reliable source. They had not 'snubbed' the offer, as Railton suggested, but dismissed allegations that the offer had been made to them. It was sad that none of the Press reported that the crew volunteered to accept McDonald's offer on Wednesday, but that McDonald had by then withdrawn his offer, explaining that it had had a time limit which lasted until Tuesday midnight, a deadline they had missed. By the end of the week, the daily papers were divided in their opinions: Dodd appeared to be talking to at least some of the involved parties, giving the impression of a two-sided argument; Railton in *The Times* was still latching on to the time limit of the dispute, selecting the issues which bothered the Establishment most of all, whilst Matheson continued to paraphrase, pass comment and not explain the situation.

By sheer weight of repetition, the picture clear to the readership was something like this: the major dispute was between Clark, a disreputable Californian oarsman who had failed to complete most of the training requirements, and McDonald the President, a quiet, mild-mannered chap who had trained hard all year, but had been beaten in a Seat Race by the Californian. But McDonald was in charge, and had every right to select the crew and, since he had beaten Clark on several occasions on something called an ergometer, he deserved a place because most of the coaches said so. That Clark was an American and Californian and a brat was clear, but exactly who else is involved wasn't. The others seemed to be Americans too, except for this guy called Ward who also, like McDonald, wanted Clark's seat. Cambridge had no sympathy with Oxford, who had a problem 'of their own making', and the President, Steve Peel, assured McDonald that they would only race a crew selected by him.

The misunderstanding reverberating around the British Press was somewhat understandable when you realise that by the middle of the second week of the dispute none of the reporters had spoken to the oarsmen involved, and few had spoken to the coaches, although all had heard McDonald's statements to the Press, underlining his interpretation of the Boat Club's problems and how he would go about solving them. Chris Dodd told me he had been reporting the dispute blind from Manchester in the early half of the week because he was there writing a report on another story. His absence from the scene of the events and the confusion amongst the reporters probably explains Dodd's biggest gaffe in his report on Wednesday, 28 January, where he suggested that: 'The way toward a compromise would be for McDonald to put himself on the bank and give Clark a bowside seat on probation.' This would have solved nothing. It would have left them a person short on strokeside and left Ward out on bowside!

While Dodd was in Manchester, he received a call from Jon Fish, asking him to come to Oxford to talk to them because they felt they were being unfairly represented in the Press. Dodd arranged to return to London via Oxford and meet Fish outside Oriel. Fish took him to a room nearby in a college annexe, and, to his surprise, most of the Blue Boat squad were present. McDonald and Cadoux-Hudson were not there and nor was Clark, but Lyons, Huntington, Penney, Stewart, Ward and Hull were. Dodd listened to their explanation of events and complaints about the conduct of the club and the handling of matters in the Press, but was at a loss when they asked him what they should do next. His only advice to them was to decide what they wanted to do and to say so clearly. 'I told them it was my job to report on the dispute, not to tell them what to do, even if I knew. But I advised them to decide what they wanted to do and say so step by step, and that they would have to find a solution which would enable the other side to save face, whoever was right or wrong. I pointed out that making lengthy proclamations of principle to reporters who knew nothing about OUBC, the Boat Race or rowing was a recipe for disaster in respect of a paragraph or two which would eventually appear.'

Dodd told me that it was obvious to him that they were not prepared for the course of events thus far. 'That was one of the reasons why they were getting a bad Press. They didn't have a strategy, they sort of knew what they believed but there was no organised plot, and they hadn't had a chance to explain themselves.'

Dodd also met Clark that day in University College. Clark talked to Dodd off the record, but was refusing to speak to other reporters. He told Dodd that what he wanted now was to get on with his work. He said that whatever happened now, he was out of it. Dodd's recollection is that he said that the ball was now in McDonald's court and that he, Clark, didn't want to be the cause of any more trouble.

Following his meetings with Clark and with the others, and a statement given by Huntington in Oriel Square, Dodd was able to print his own interpretation of the run of events over the last two weeks. He tried to combine the story from both sides to sum up the dispute. He listed twelve steps in the dispute, starting with the niggling Seat Race which sparked it off. In his article he said that Clark beat McDonald in a Seat Race, as did Matheson in a report in *The Independent,* 28 January, where he agreed that 'Clark had been the victor by 2/3rds of a length'. Later, Dodd told me that it was 'almost impossible to work out whether the Seat Race was fixed, or not.' Matheson obviously believed that the race was rigged by Clark's American friends. Trying to act as a mediator and coach in the following week, he talked to the oarsmen and suggested to them that 'all oarsmen cheat in Seat Races', and then went on to explain a situation in the 1976 World Championship crew which Freddie Smallbone had been stroking. Matheson said they didn't want him in the crew because the crew went better with the other guy, they thought. So they just didn't pull 'quite as hard in the race for Freddie'. 'He was giving us a chance to justify our action,' Penney told me, 'but it really disgusted us that anybody would suggest that we would fake the results of a Seat Race just so that we could row with our buddies.'

Penney in particular was angered by the accusations. He was the other stroke, and was the one who was being criticised for cheating. A comment which has been thrown in my direction time and time again was with regard to

Penney's personal integrity: 'Is there any guy in the world with more integrity than Penney?' Fish, Lyons and Stewart asked me, and the answer from everybody who knows him was 'NO!' The query definitely wasn't who won the race, because all present agreed that Clark's crew was in front. The allegations were that he hadn't really won it, because his American friends cheated in the race by pulling for Clark but not for McDonald, allegations they hotly deny. And secondly, that the Seat Race was irrelevant because Clark had been beaten by McDonald on other occasions, and thus one test did not justify his place in the crew. After talking to them, Dodd concentrated on the crew's requests. He pointed out for the first time that 'Their main demand was to have a fair trial to determine whether the inclusion of the President, Donald McDonald, or the sacked Californian would make the boat move faster' (*The Guardian,* Saturday, 31 January).

The day before Dodd's article, Railton quoted McDonald as suggesting that the two sides were 'Operating the same criteria, that you go for the fastest crew, but it just happens there are two versions of what constitutes the fastest crew' (*The Times,* Friday, 30 January), and although he didn't quote him saying it there, McDonald had said in an earlier article, published in *The Guardian,* that he was the man for the job. 'The great majority of the coaches – 95% – backed me. They know I am the guy for the boat. I know it. I don't have a problem about that. . .' (*The Guardian,* Wednesday, 28 January).

With the backing of the coaches, McDonald wasn't interested in any more trials, even though originally the crew had been announced only as a provisional squad, and there would have been more trials anyway, and despite his opponents' later attempts to bait him into demonstrating his worth against Clark. 'If McDonald is in fact better than Clark, he should not have any difficulty proving it to the rest of the squad' (*The Times,* 7 February, 1987).

Clark had his first say in *The Times* on Thursday, 29 January, when he tried to instil the idea that the dispute was not a rebellion. 'It involves the whole crew. . . it appears to be a battle between the Establishment and us, but it is not, we are just seeking a compromise. . .' (*The*

Times, 29 January).

Stewart spoke too that day, but to *The Guardian:* 'Our actions have always been taken as a crew,' he said, 'and we have not been American-led. We wish to maintain our integrity and that of the Oxford University Boat Club by producing the fastest possible crew' (*The Guardian,* 29 January).

With many of Britain's respected voices of rowing speaking out, the guys didn't seem to have much of a chance: whatever they said would be counteracted by another report with quotes from someone 'important'. For example, Richard Burnell, who rowed in 1939, and was Captain of the Great Britain Rowing Team (1950), mocked the suggestions that it wasn't purely an American-led dispute: 'The Yank comes to Oxford, not as in the famous film to rescue the crew from defeat, but to invite the President of the OUBC to step aside to allow the outsider to row in his preferred position in the crew,' he said, without trying to explain what it is that makes Clark an outsider. After all, the Boat Race is for students of all races and nationalities, not just for the British. This article did not maintain any consistency with the articles he has since written glorifying the presence of foreigners who have shaken up the Boat Club in years past. One particularly notable occasion was in his description of his years of rowing for Oxford. In the Boat Race programme for the 1989 race, Burnell wrote:

> 'In 1939, Oxford had just emerged from a run of defeats. . . but it was an Australian, Jock Lewes, who was elected as President of the OUBC in 1937, who turned Oxford rowing upside down, which was something appropriate for an Aussie, and therapeutic for those concerned on the Isis.'

Burnell admits that it can take a foreigner to give the club a new sense of direction, that their methods are not always appreciated initially, but that these efforts could be very refreshing. It is a shame that he did not cast his mind back to his rowing days before he wrote the rest of his condemnatory article in 1987. He goes on: 'Of course, this particular Yank, Chris Clark, totally denies he is the ringleader, whilst providing all the evidence that he is.' Burnell doesn't say what evidence exactly, but I guess that he, like other old Blues, gleaned his information from the confused coaches and from fellow journalists, who it seems never really got to the bottom of the dispute, but were happier interesting their readership in debating a series of topical discussions which have surrounded the Boat Race for years. One would have thought that these tiresome backbench debates could have waited until after they had solved the present dilemma. Following quotes from the Cambridge President, Peel, and the Cambridge coaches, suggesting that Oxford had recruited the Americans purely to row in the Boat Race, something Cambridge would never do, the allegations in *The Independent* and *The Guardian,* that Clark had brought the other Americans over here to row, the first line of debate was the obvious one of whether recruiting post-graduate International sportsmen on Mickey Mouse courses to boost the Boat Race line-up should be allowed to happen. Noticeably, everyone assumed it did and that it was a part of the race these days, particularly since losing in 1986 had made Clark publicly vow at the Boat Race Ball to return and 'kick Cambridge's ass', even if he had to bring the whole US squad with him to do it. It was possibly the most quoted saying during the whole dispute; it seemed so fitting for the occasion, and made many feel that Clark had done just that, and that the other Americans were here only because of him. To think that one oarsman's after-the-Race dreams (particularly the tantrum-prone Clark) should have the authority to convince the rowing coaches and the college tutors that these Americans were needed here to ensure Cambridge's downfall is particularly quaint, and, I might say, rather flattering to Clark and particularly unflattering to the Oxford College dons, who would be the laughing stock of the University if true. However, despite this rather bizarre claim, it gave Cambridge the chance to voice their thoughts, and they made it quite clear that such recruiting is not something that they take part in, because they don't think it's good for the Race (nor sensible for either University).

Meanwhile, Simon Barnes, freelance reporter for *The Times,* suggested that: 'Next year, perhaps Oxford will bring in Dennis O'Connor, giving him a perfectly genuine place on his academic merits to read astro-physics. . . and in his spare moments he can cox the Oxford Boat Race.' Suggestions like this did nothing to help the dispute, but helped to sustain public interest in a healthy debate on the stature of the great Boat Race. Another favourite topic became the Yankees just not understanding our British traditions. McDonald added credit to this one by suggesting that they 'don't, you see, understand the special traditions of the Boat Race. . . they think it's quaint but forget that it is still a very big important race' (*The Guardian,* 31 January).

This comment was sure to bring a great response, as there are many British individuals who will seek to defend the British institutions that Americans just don't understand. Mr R B Lockhart wrote a letter to *The Times,* suggesting that we needed to teach 'Ageing Yank permanent students a thing or two about the institution which is our Boat Race. They also might learn that to many of us, a sporting contest in a pleasant and gentlemanly manner can matter more than their imported win-at-all-costs principles, or their personal wounded pride' (*The Times,* 4 February). Mr Lockhart was maybe a little confused, since both sides were prepared to 'win at all costs', although whether the dispute or the Boat Race was more important to win had become a little clouded. Ironically, the very argument of the Americans' case was based upon the integrity of the selection process, which, in their opinion, should be conducted in an honest and fair-minded fashion – the very principles that make up 'gentlemanly' behaviour. Mr Lockhart can, however, be excused his confusion, since his information presumably came from the Press, and his interests were seemingly in true sportsmanship. I cannot feel the same sympathy for journalist Mick Brown, who suggested that the very idea 'Of the American rowers coming to Oxford to lecture on ethics may also strike some as trifle rich, particularly given the popular assumption that their main reason for being here is for the privilege of rowing in the Boat Race' (1 February).

In fact, McDonald was the very person to give evidence to suggest this wasn't true. He obviously felt that the Americans were there to row and do nothing else when he told Steve Kiesling, reporter for the *New Yorker,* that 'They came here to row, and then they got caught up in their studies – rowing is the quintessential Oxford experience, work is secondary.' I'm not sure that the Oxford tutors would agree, nor would the Americans themselves, who were adamant all the way through that half the problem with the Boat Race was that it took too much time unnecessarily, making conscientious study very difficult. They were there to row, but they were also there to get their individual qualifications, and saw both as important. Perhaps McDonald had forgotten the demands of academia, having taken a year out from his studies to concentrate on being President of the Boat Club, and expected his crew, who were in the midst of their study, to do likewise. In the following year, Fish spoke many times on the importance of maintaining a healthy balance between academic life, sporting life and social demands which fill a student's under/post-graduate career. The healthy balance is something which the student may find difficult to stay in charge of, particularly in the case of a Boat Race which has assumed so much importance that it may begin to take absolute priority over everything. This he sees as a recipe for disaster, something which many college tutors will heartily agree with. Following the introduction of this balance by the Boat Club in 1988, Steve Royle, now professional Director of the Oxford University Rowing Club, has tried hard to maintain the distinction between the time rowing takes and the time allotted to study. He has attempted to prevent the common misconception which the Americans became a party to, that rowers go to Oxford *just* to row. They may go because it's a great place to row whilst studying, but there are better places to row if that's all they have in mind; for the academic, however, there are few better places to study.

14

There was a problem with authority during the dispute; the question of whose authority was gospel was a stumbling block. Theoretically, McDonald as President had the authority to make any decision he wished. However, he obviously wanted some support when it came to dropping Clark. In the first instance, he turned to his coaches, particularly Topolski, who had been Boat Race coach for ten consecutive Oxford wins. He was very highly respected in the eyes of the University, the public, other coaches and many oarsmen and women around the country. Unfortunately though, Topolski's and McDonald's authority was questioned when Mike Spracklen, then Britain's Chief Coach, refused to put his signature to Clark's elimination from the Boat Club. Any weak link in the resolve of the coaching team was bound to lower the credibility of their decision. Total support from his coaching team was something that Topolski had hoped he could count on, and there is no doubt that non-compliance, particularly from Spracklen, bugged him. Had the lack of co-operation come from any other member of the coaching team, there would not have been a problem, but Spracklen had a name as a coach and a record of success greater than Topolski's. He has tremendous International stature as a coach and as a man of great integrity. He coaches the cream of the sport, and so he is not as well-known to non-rowers as Topolski is because of his Boat Race success (the Boat Race is a commercial event), but Spracklen has world-wide acclaim and a tremendous credibility with those who row. Topolski and the oarsmen were aware of Spracklen's importance, and knew that if he spoke out against the management of the dispute, others might too.

Topolski wanted to feel happy about the decision to banish Clark from the crew, and was ready to defend Spracklen's difference of opinion. He refers to Spracklen as a 'true artist of the sport' but clarifies that his talents are best when directed to coaching oarsmen in two-thousand-metre, six-lane racing. Topolski makes it clear he doesn't consider him a Boat Race specialist. Topolski's run of successive wins over his thirteen years as coach gives authority to his statement, particularly since his influence has revived the Boat Race madness which entices support to the race. Topolski's classification of rowing coaches into Boat Race specialists and two-thousand-metre race specialists may seem justified considering Topolski's long run of success, but there is plenty of evidence to suggest that there is a certain amount of poetic licence in his suggestion! Between 1890 and 1898, when Oxford had nine consecutive wins, and between 1924 and 1936, when Cambridge won thirteen consecutive races, neither University was coached continually by one particular Boat Race specialist: both Universities were directed by several coaches. Many of these were also the coaches of the British National rowing team, who raced sprint and two-thousand-metre races in the summer months, as today's National team does. Thus, it would seem strange that after over a hundred years of Boat Race crews being coached by coaches who coached top class Internationals as well, that Topolski should try and lay claim that there is a difference between producing a crew for one race and a crew for another. A good coach will know how to prepare any crew for any important race. The training regimes will differ slightly because of the nature of the race, but the methods of preparing the oarsmen, improving their rowing technique and preparing them as a crew for the race, is very much the same. It is ludicrous to suggest that those who spend most of their time preparing crews for two-thousand-metre races or those who have not rowed the Boat Race, or have not been to Oxford or Cambridge, cannot possibly coach and produce a Boat Race crew.

When Spracklen made his point that Clark was a potentially brilliant oarsman who was already of international standing, and that McDonald wasn't and was never likely to be, he was making an objective statement based upon his knowledge of the two men's individual ability. He made the decision before he really understood the politics, and was prepared to stand by his statement because he thought that the politics were clouding the real issue. 'McDonald,' he said, 'was the nice guy, but personality has to be irrelevant in international sport; the ones who try the hardest aren't always the ones to succeed. He is a good top club oarsman who trains very hard, but when I was asked who was better, my answer was Clark.' Topolski insisted that Clark was not the best man for the Boat Race, adamant that Spracklen's judgement was based upon two-thousand-metre races not the Boat Race, and he was frustrated by Spracklen's refusal to agree with him.

Their disagreement generated a lot of Press interest because Spracklen's opinion sided with the oarsmen's. This was particularly so when he openly refuted the statement which McDonald had given to the Press after the Leander meeting, which said that it was a 'unanimous' agreement to drop Clark. Spracklen said it was not unanimous, but that an 'overwhelming majority' had supported the selection of McDonald over Clark. He had no axe to grind against any of the coaches or the oarsmen, but objected to the use of lies to further their cause. In *The Times,* Railton quoted Spracklen as saying that 'he understood the grievances of several members of the crew. . . It is,' he pointed out, 'the mentality of the top class oarsman who, like everybody else, is trying to find the fastest crew' (*The Times,* 27 January).

'Spracklen was wrong to speak out in this way,' said Mark Lees, and Royle agreed. They felt that Spracklen was undermining the authority of the coaching team talking to the Press and refuting McDonald's statement. Lees said that during the meeting they were all asked to stand by a majority decision and all of them, Spracklen included, said they would. By refuting the President's Press statement, they felt that he did a lot of damage, and in fact went as far as to suggest that this open disagreement was to blame for the continuation of the dispute. Lees is probably right; one of the reasons that the dispute did rumble on was because of this difference in opinion. But Spracklen did not refute the decision, he merely corrected the inaccuracies in the Press report. He had made it quite clear before he entered the meeting that his loyalties lay with the oarsmen, and that it was the President who released a deceitful report. If Spracklen had not spoken out, he would have been unfair to the oarsmen, who he had already told that Clark was the best man. Spracklen was not concerned with loyalty but with integrity. There was a case for disagreement in the Boat Club, and it should have been resolved by solving the dilemma, not by one side making it impossible for the other to compete. Integrity became a big issue in this dispute. As Mick Brown, reporter for *The Sunday Times,* said: 'This is not simply a story of brash Americans attempting to usurp a hallowed British institution. It is a question of integrity. Whose integrity is a little difficult to unravel' (*The Sunday Times,* 1 February, 1987). By speaking out, Spracklen questioned the integrity, not of their collective decision to drop Clark, but the integrity of a President who felt he had to lie to ensure his complete control: he did not want to be involved in that sort of deception. His was the only published demonstration of support that the crew had had from any member of the coaching team or the University. In contrast, by the middle of the second week of the dispute, the President had the support of most of his coaching team, many old Blues and numerous offers from other University oarsmen to row, should the present Blue Boat continue to refuse to comply with his wishes. And he had his Boat Club Constitution, which gave him power to do just about anything he wanted to.

He had legal power, Establishment support and his own determination. The mutineers had only justice, morality and Spracklen on their side. It seems they should have taken heed of Machiavelli's old warning, 'that there is nothing more difficult to carry out, more dangerous to handle than to initiate a new order of things. For the informer has enemies in all who would profit by the old order and only lukewarm defenders in all who would profit by the new.'

The oarsmen had begun at long last to see things in perspective; once Isis had agreed to row, they began to realise that they had been naive about the whole thing. 'It was the beginning of the end of a lot of idealism in my life,' said Lyons retrospectively. 'We actually thought that people would listen to our cries of foul play, but they didn't because McDonald was more prepared than we were. He made every move first, and by the time we'd prepared any form of counter-attack it was always too late.' It wasn't until McDonald's sudden withdrawal of his offer to stand down from the crew if Clark did too, that finally goaded them into action. Until then, they hadn't realised that they were playing a stragegy game in which McDonald had the upper hand. Their belief in human nature had made them slow on the uptake. Their lack of preparation to make certain their arguments were heard surely disproves claims that their arguments were made as a premeditated attempt to overthrow the Boat Club.

Their first planned action was an attempt to get everyone rowing again with some semblance of acceptability for both sides. To do this, Clark offered to resign his place in the crew if McDonald would offer his resignation as President and let Stewart stand in his place. That way, McDonald could still row and, without McDonald actually in charge, they all felt that Clark would be able to remain involved with the crew in an organisational capacity. It wasn't the soluution that they hoped for, but they agreed that the bitterness was so deep on both sides that the most anyone could expect now was for a compromise. Clark is no fool: he sensed that the issue had become so centred around him that he would never have a chance of further selection trials. He was the first to ask the others to go back and row. Clark suffered badly from the personal attacks, but was given solace by his fellow oarsmen's insistence on seeing justice done. They saw no reason for Clark to be made a scapegoat, and tried hard to somehow vindicate any sacrifice Clark might have to make to restore peace. Once they had agreed to accept Clark's offer to stand down, 'They even suggested,' said

Clark, 'that I could get involved with the coaching of the crew if McDonald wasn't President, which was kind of bizarre, but would've been fun.' Not only was it 'bizarre', it would have been very unpopular and would have caused a lot of outrage had it happened! Clark didn't tell McDonald about this suggestion, although I expect it made it easier for Clark to offer this compromise knowing that he could still be involved. He was in a difficult position: he didn't want anybody not to row because of him, and although it was their own choice, he felt responsible. 'Just because he is the sort of person who would take the guilt,' said Fish, 'we kept reassuring him that our stance was not just for him but for Ward, for reason and for fairness too; but it was hard for Clark, because the whole of Britain was telling him he'd ruined the Boat Race, and he didn't want to be remembered for that. He was even getting hate mail suggesting he should leave the country by the fastest possible means! That is a lot of hate for any one person to shoulder. We were all having a hard time, a really hard time, McDonald included, but it was by choice that we stuck it out. For Clark, it was by everybody else's choice; he was having not only his rowing ability challenged, but his whole personality, and he could do nothing about it.'

Clark met McDonald over a drink in the Eastgate Hotel in Oxford, safely hidden from inquisitive reporters. The get-together was strange for them both, but Clark remembers it as very calm. They discussed Clark's proposal, but came to no agreement. 'He didn't trust me,' Clark laughed. 'He thought that once he'd resigned as President there would be repercussions on his place; funnily enough, we hadn't even thought of that, our plan to put me in as part of the coaching team was far more tame!'

The next day the Press reports the two men had released once again emphasised the battering each side was prepared to give the other. Clark reported that McDonald had refused to accept the offer, for fear of 'admitting defeat', whilst McDonald reported that Clark had told him he had no further wish to row in the race, and wished his colleagues to row for Oxford. Both statements were personal interpretations designed to singe the opposition. This was equivalent to political dog-fighting, both sides looking for majority support to further wound the opposition.

It was a great shame that this proposal failed, and it angered the oarsmen that McDonald was prepared to fight on. Equally, it annoyed McDonald that they wouldn't come back and row. 'It bothers me that they should throw it up for the sake of a misguided principle,' he told Chris Dodd. Comments like this only made the crew more determined to accept nothing less than rowing in the fastest possible crew. McDonald, I think, had lost all vision of being in the fastest crew; all he wanted now was a crew to row with who had no doubt in his personal ability, and with Isis he had such a crew. With Tom Cadoux-Hudson and himself to make up the numbers, he had the makings of a fairly 'normal' University crew, without the added trimmings of five current American Internationals. McDonald could only hope that the threat of the Boat Race happening without them would be enough to bring the absent oarsmen back with their tails between their legs.

McDonald issued another deadline on Thursday, 29 January, the day after his meeting with Isis and his drink with Clark. Guaranteed a crew, he gave all members of the Boat Club until Sunday midnight to pledge their availability to row. Meanwhile, the Press were once again trying to stay one step ahead of the dispute; they decided that the crew weren't going to go back unless they could see their disagreements as pointless.

'The dissidents are sacrificing much of what they had trained for, and will gain nothing once this flurry of interest has died' (*The Independent,* 30 January). It was a plea for them to return: people were saying that they were crazy to continue when it was obvious that McDonald wasn't going to give in. Forget your differences and row, was their advice. Matheson, coach and reporter, felt, as did many in the rowing world, powerless to intercede and sad that they were not to row. Kiesling, reporter for the *New Yorker,* himself an oarsman who had been prevented from going to the Moscow Olympics because of Government politics, remembered the heartache that it caused him. He compared this Oxford boycott to the one which was forced upon him. His attitude was clear; he said nothing and nobody is worth boycotting something you have trained hard for. They had a chance of a lifetime and they missed out, which is sad. It seemed the whole world wanted them to go back and row as much as the oarsmen themselves wanted to go back and row. Nobody understood how or why they continued, but then nobody at the time knew the full story. Steve Royle remembered how much they all wanted to row, and how it hurt him to see the dispute ending like this. He, like so many others, was upset by the bitterness and anger which caused them to refuse to row. He didn't, like some, label them as ridiculous for continuing to stand by their judgement, and didn't comment on the apparent lack of power that the coaches had to persuade a compromise. It is a pity that his sympathies, along with his feeling that it was for the students to sort out this dispute alone, wasn't matched by every other person who somehow felt the need to give their opinion or advice.

In a final attempt to find a solution they looked to the only people who had any authority over the President: the College Boat Captains who had helped to vote McDonald in as President back in the summer term of 1986. They were playing with real politics now, putting their case to the majority vote. They cannot claim to have thought of the idea themselves: McDonald had already approached the Captains at their regular meeting two weeks before, and had suggested that they give him a vote of confidence, although a statement given on 2 February, 1987, by 28 of the Captains to *The Guardian,* reported that 'no vote of confidence was given to McDonald two weeks ago.' The oarsmen could see that the only clear way for them to have more trials was to force McDonald out of his Presidency, but to do that they needed some support. They sent a letter to the Captains of Boats of each College to ascertain their feelings. What they discovered was encouraging: many of the Captains seemed horrified at the mess they were witnessing, and were eager to find out exactly what was happening. Six of those Captains volunteered to request an extraordinary meeting of the College Captains, to discuss the President's handling of the interests of the

OUBC and the crew. A letter was forwarded to McDonald's College, requesting a meeting to take place on Sunday night, before McDonald's deadline. McDonald, however, knowing his powers, convened the meeting for the following Tuesday, saying smugly that it should take place. The strategy game was rearing its ugly head again.

Oxford was bubbling with the pros and cons of Presidential rule, the whys and wherefores of having graduates rowing in the Boat Race, the mismanagement or not of the Boat Club, McDonald's virtues and his iron ruling, Topolski's importance, and all in anticipation of a meeting convened to make public history. Either McDonald would go down through a vote of no confidence, although nobody seemed sure what that would mean, or the crew would have to decide whether the Boat Race would happen without Oxford's fastest seven men. Because of the Sunday deadline and McDonald's choice of a following Tuesday meeting, all the oarsmen except Lyons and Fish phoned McDonald to say they would row. Lyons and Fish felt they should not be seen to support the President at all, and the others felt it worthwhile keeping their options open until after the Captains' meeting.

An outing was arranged for the Tuesday afternoon at Henley under the guidance of Hugh Matheson, the appointed coach for the next two weeks. The newspaper reporters who didn't know better saw a crew afloat and reported the end of the mutiny. Matheson was anxious to keep his crew away from the Press, and tried to lay a false trail to keep them away. Having grouped with the oarsmen in Oriel Square, he set off at breakneck speeds through the narrow streets of Oxford with Dodd in the passenger seat saying a few Hail Marys for his sins. 'Hugh thought he'd shake off the TV crew and photographers by driving off in the opposite direction to the OUBC minibus. The TV crew followed him, and a cops-and-robbers chase ensued, ending with the TV Volvo lost somewhere in the back streets of East Oxford, and Hugh arriving at Henley via the M40 and Remenham Hill. The photographers, meanwhile, had followed the OUBC van which had picked up the boat trailer and led a convoy — including the TV crew — across Henley bridge to

Leander, as Hugh arrived from the other direction,' Dodd told me.

Geoffrey Page, casting his experienced eye over the crew that boated, remarked poignantly what a tragedy it would be if Oxford lost the talent that was out in the crew that day for the sake of a domestic quarrel. He, like many other fanatical Boat Race supporters, wanted to see a fast crew race for Oxford. What a pity all those eminent rowing journalists did not think of that in the beginning, for then it might have remained 'just a domestic quarrel'.

The following day, the private arguments went public again, following the Captains' meeting held at New College. The previous day's hopeful reports of a resolved dispute were cast aside as the five Americans didn't turn up for training. The Captains' meeting had not been a success for them, as a vote of confidence in McDonald had been passed: 28 votes for and 11 against. Evidence, I hear you say, that the oarsmen were wrong. However, a similar vote two weeks later at the Oxford Union voted in the other direction: 152 votes for the motion that 'the OUBC has mishandled the organisation of the Boat Race crew', and 10 against! The difference in the two meetings was mainly due to a difference in structure which further demonstrated the uncanny and manipulative power an Establishment has over individuals. The Union is a debating chamber where two balanced sides debate an issue in front of an audience, who then decide upon the evidence, and by the way it is portrayed to them, which side they believe is right. Individuals attend the debates with the desire to ascertain rights and wrongs. Their decisions carry no immediate effect, and thus there is no reservation to do the right thing or follow the grain. The Captains' meeting, however, was a law unto itself: McDonald chaired the meeting, having already taken copious amounts of advice from his friend and lawyer, Simon Barnes, with regard to the format of the meeting and the questions and accusations he should and should not allow. Topolski, Fishlock and Dr Barry were present to provide emotional and authoritative support. Clark and Stewart were the only members of the crew present, not by choice, but because McDonald started the meeting in a dictatorial manner by instructing anyone in the room not present in an official capacity to leave; Clark was present representing St. Johns College Boat Club, and Stewart appeared in his capacity as Vice-President of the University Boat Club.

McDonald anticipated the tone the meeting would take. He realised that the rowers would rely on the emotive power of the few Captains who felt very strongly that the crew had been cheated, to put across their arguments and provide the majority of the Captains (who didn't have a clue what was going on), with enough information to give the impression that the crew were being hard done by. I was there as President of the Women's Boat Club, and I didn't rate their chances very highly, particularly as their spokesmen started out in a very forthright, outraged manner which was not good psychologically at such a meeting.

The majority of the Captains obviously felt that they were being asked to make a very important decision, which of course they were: the President of the OUBC had never lost his place through a vote of 'no confidence' before, and McDonald made this very clear and pointed out the responsibility they were undertaking, stressing the seriousness and rationality that should prevail. They wanted answers to their questions, and they wanted to be sure any vote taken was in the best interests of the University. Angry retorts, or any sign of defensive behaviour from McDonald or any of the coaches might have been enough to pave the way for a vote of no confidence. But McDonald and his coaches remained calm throughout. Only Topolski could not resist the temptation to shout back. But the crew-supporting Captains were on the wrong tack. The accusations were flying at Topolski, and his increasing distress kept them coming, but Topolsk wasn't leading this dispute, McDonald was. As long as they could prevent an early call for a vote of no confidence, the outrage would die down; and as McDonald refused to take a request from the floor for a motion calling a vote, time was on his side. It was the voice of Michael Suarez, a Jesuit priest from Campion Hall and a long-time personal friend of McDonald's, who brought to the floor the apparent voice of reason and rationality which many of the Captains were looking for. Had everybody there been aware of his deep-seated connections with McDonald, I doubt very much that his oratorical skills would have been as potent as they were.

There is no doubt that Suarez was not the independent voice he was made out to be, under the guise of a lacrosse player and Boat Club Captain of Campion Hall. He launched into a soul-searching attack on Clark that made him out to be a detriment to the 'University, his sport and the United States of America'. Suarez's soliloquy painted a damning portrait of Clark that was rather similar to the one the newspapers had given him since McDonald's first statements. According to Suarez, Clark was a dodgy character with only his own interests in mind, a man who had managed to lead the whole meeting astray. 'It was only fair that Clark and his gang should appeal against McDonald's decision to drop him from the boat, since there was a potential conflict of interest. But who are we to contest the opinion, not merely of McDonald himself, but of the overwhelming majority of Oxford's coaches?' he remonstrated to his audience. He spoke with the power of a man who was sure of his facts. Even though his facts were incorrect, his speech was convincing. Suarez didn't mention that Clark was in the crew on one day then dropped the next, or why Ward wasn't good enough and then was. He didn't reiterate the coaches' change of heart at the St. Giles House meeting which resulted in McDonald taking authority into his own hands, nor did he mention the indisputable fact that the selection had been mismanaged. Disputes of this intensity don't just happen: one only has to look to the French or recent East European Revolutions to see how desperate individuals have to become before feelings of unrest stimulate a revolution to fruition!

Suarez was convincing, and when he finished his speech the meeting was effectively over. Stewart tried to stop the galloping corrosion which had set in, but his words fell upon deaf ears. There was little he could do to convince the Captains that Suarez was just another part of the deception. They needed someone like Spracklen to stand

and proclaim 'victimisation' in his hushed, authoritarian voice. Only someone with his commanding nature could have challenged this orator. Once again, apparent authority and reason clouded the issue.

Bruce Philp (President 1986) closed the meeting by requesting a vote, and thus McDonald was duly granted the confidence of his Captains. Stewart and Clark left the meeting in a fit of frustration, realising that once again they would leave a 'public hearing' without having successfully portrayed the depth of their feelings and the true story behind the dispute. The result of that meeting ended the Boat Race rowing careers of the five Americans for 1987. The oarsmen had failed to make their story heard; Isis, along with Cadoux-Hudson and McDonald, would be representing Oxford in the Boat Race. The Americans refused any requests for them to go back and row in McDonald's crew because they said that they were horrified by 'the injustice' of the whole dispute, and could not tolerate being a part of it. Their British crewmates, Ward, Hull and Stewart did go back, all for very personal reasons, a move which further established the idea of the dispute being an 'American mutiny'.

15

The new Blue Boat was not a crew to be scoffed at, despite lacking the impressive list of rowing qualifications the Americans had. All the crew members were competent oarsmen and had their own share of talent and wins: Andy Lobbenburg, Isis cox 1986, would be steering the crew; Tom Cadoux-Hudson, a World Bronze medallist in the Coxed Pairs; Richard Hull rowed at Cambridge for three years; Gavin Stewart stroked Isis to victory in 1986; Paul Gleeson, the man recommended by McDonald to take his place when he offered to stand down; Pete Gish, an American who had previously rowed for Dartmouth College, USA; Tony Ward, junior international and Isis 1986; Hugh Pelham, also Isis 1986; and, of course, McDonald, who had rowed in the 1986 Blue Boat.

Only Hull, Ward and Stewart had been deeply involved in the crisis of the last few weeks, although they had had a lot of support from Gish, Cadoux-Hudson and Gleeson, and there was, suffice to say, a lot of hard feeling within the crew about the way the dispute had been handled. Their decisions to return and row with McDonald were made in very emotional circumstances. Their distrust, despondency and hatred at the way the dispute had been ended, and the constant press attention, had obviously taken its toll and made it extremely difficult for the guys to look clearly at the prospect of preparing for the Boat Race over the next seven weeks. It took courage for them to subdue that unpleasantness. Stewart resigned his Vice-Presidency before agreeing to return under OUBC rule, a symbolic act to demonstrate his disappointment in the way things had been handled. He felt he had to return and row for the

University, despite his disappointment at the way things had been run. His reasons for returning were, he said, 'too personal to discuss'. On the other hand, Hull and Ward were dogmatic when they explained why they had gone back to row after enduring the weeks of fighting for a principle. 'The argument was lost,' Ward told me. 'If we hadn't gone back to row then Isis would've rowed and I couldn't bear the thought of that. We made it clear what we thought was right, and what was wrong; there was nothing more to gain by not rowing. What was important now was to win the Boat Race and to make our mark by winning our Blues.' Each one made a personal decision about whether or not they should return to the crew. The fact that none of the Americans returned and all the Britons did will label the dispute as an American one for years to come.

The Americans remained very bitter, particularly Huntington and Penney, who felt more and more despair as the dispute deepened. They could not return, not because of pride but because they felt strongly that they did not want to row in the crew which had been unfairly selected. 'They took the brunt of the press criticism, which made it very nationalistic; that made it easier for us to go back but harder for them,' explained Ward. Many suggested they didn't go back because an Oxford Rowing Blue and the Boat Race did not mean enough to them, and because they didn't understand or feel any empathy with our great tradition. The award of a Rowing Blue to the Americans meant something different than it did to their English crewmates. To Ward, Hull and Stewart, apart from the honour associated with the award, it represented achieving a recognised standard of oarsmanship, but the Americans had already far surpassed that standard; they had already achieved international recognition. Four of them had World or Olympic medals. Those medals were symbols of their oarsmanship, a Rowing Blue meant something different to them – it was a trophy which represented the ideals of the Boat Race. To have been party to those ideals was the importance of a Rowing Blue. Their dedication to the sport and the Boat Race was never in doubt. Rowing in the race meant a lot to them, rowing in the fastest crew possible meant a lot to them, and being a part of true amateur sport meant a lot to them. But it didn't mean so much that they would sacrifice absolutely everything to do it. They wanted to be a part of the Boat Race and to win the race, but not at all costs. If you believe that there is a right way and a wrong way to do things then you will understand; if you believe that the means justify the end, then you will not. Few people will ever properly understand their reasons for holding out and not rowing; disgust and disbelief were the main ones and, although the bitterness has worn away with time, if you ever have the opportunity to talk with any of the oarsmen involved, you will still feel their disbelief. You feel also their sadness that it was such an unpleasant dispute.

Having made their final decision not to accept McDonald's terms, they tried to leave the Boat Club well alone. They were still in day-to-day contact with most of the crew; after all, they were good friends, but apart from social contact they were happy to leave well alone. They continued rowing and coaching but concentrated their efforts on College rowing for Torpids and Summer Bumps Races. But for the main part they were happy to step back from the pressures of the public eye and piece together their academic and rowing careers which had been hastily put aside during those few weeks. The despondency which they felt at not rowing (although justified to themselves by a clear conscience), was paralleled by the despondency which Hugh Matheson and Topolski were trying to combat in the new Blue Boat. They were sad at having lost the Americans, and unenthused by the speed of the new crew – Hull likened it to driving a Mini after a Rolls-Royce! Everyone was drained after weeks of argument and reproach, and the camaraderie that normally accompanies a crew was just not there. 'There were too many forces pulling us apart,' Hull told me. 'The attitude wasn't good, but then there was no reason for it to be. We were all rowing for very different reasons, harbouring very different feelings for one another.' Coaches, friends, family and old Blues alike were all painfully aware of the difficulty these men faced. They had to beat their own feelings before they could even begin to think of conquering Cambridge. 'The real things we had going for ourselves were that we had rowed, trained with and Seat Raced the Americans all year, and I think because of that, individually we had confidence in ourselves and in one another. All we really needed was the confidence to put aside everything that had happened in the last few weeks. We needed to realise what a waste of effort racing would be if we lost,' said Stewart. 'We didn't get that feeling until the last week, then all of a sudden it really mattered whether we won or not.'

The tiredness and despondency of the new crew quickly led to pleas from old Blues, coaches and friends who had all felt involved in the dispute to get the Americans back. 'People seemed to think that once the publicity had died and the air calmed a little we would want to go back and row and forget everything that we had been fighting for; that was how little people understood what we had been saying and how strongly we felt,' said Fish. It was a natural desire to see things sorted out and see everybody happy. Nobody likes unhappy endings, and the threat of losing the Boat Race and the unhappiness that many could see in the Americans and in the crew lent itself to more suggestions to set everything 'right'. An emergency debate was called at the Oxford Union two Fridays after the Captains' meeting. McDonald declined to speak; he wanted to be left alone to prepare for the Boat Race. 'It is of no interest to me or to anybody in the Oxford University Boat Club,' he stated. Some considered him cowardly for not rising to the challenge to defend his management of the crew, but it would have been a brave man who, having finally resolved such a dispute and found a crew to race in, would then return to have his management challenged in front of a couple of hundred worked-up students.

In the debate the tables were turned. The crew were well represented, and although there was no shortage of individuals prepared to speak in defence of McDonald, none of them spoke with any particular authority. There were many people present who didn't appreciate the depth of feeling in the dispute. Only when the Americans finally sacrificed their chance to row in the infamous Boat Race did many really consider their side of the story. For once they had an audience prepared to listen to their side of the story, and the Americans were well prepared, their speeches were clear and well presented, and their authority clearly felt. 'On the water we are rocket fuel,' Penney told his audience. 'McDonald is a nice guy, but he is not the rocket scientist needed to control this stuff.' It was a heated debate which resulted in the House overwhelmingly supporting the motion that 'The Oxford University Boat Club has mishandled the organisation of the Boat Race Crew'. The motion was passed by 152 votes for to 10 against; thus it seems that the House believed that the Boat Club had stupidly thrown the boat's fuel overboard.

The debate had little effect on the immediate future, except to reassert that not everybody thought that the crew were the ones in the wrong, and it certainly had the effect of reopening a debate on a few questions. It is the nature of many individuals that they don't like to get involved in heated rows. These people questioned whether the dispute had been as clear-cut as the press, the President and the coaches had made it out to be, and that it was important for the future of the Boat Club. The outspokenness of old Blue and so-called mutineer from the 1959 dispute, Reed Rubin, was also important for the future of the Club. Rubin contacted Dodd through *The Guardian* to offer his services as an arbitrator, tracking him down by telephone from New York to a pub in Burford. Rubin told Dodd that if each side would nominate a representative and accept him as Chairman and that the tribunal's decision would be final, then he would come on the next available Concorde. On the day he received Rubin's offer, Dodd passed it on to William Lange, one of the five Captains involved in setting up the Captains' Meeting. He also telephoned McDonald and told him of Rubin's offer. McDonald had no idea who Rubin was, so Dodd outlined his character and credentials. Dodd described Rubin as the 'nicest man never to become President of the Oxford University Boat Club'. But despite his character reference, Dodd had the impression that the President was reluctant to consider the offer. 'His attitude was very much that it was too late to do anything like that now, and he had to be persuaded to even take down Rubin's telephone number,' Dodd said.

It was only too late because McDonald wanted it to be, since there were still nearly eight weeks left until the race.

There have been many examples of crews whose selection was not completed until a much later stage: two recent examples during Topolski's reign were, firstly, in 1978 when Dave Sawyier was President. That year the crew was not selected until the last two weeks. Equally, in 1986 the late selection of Graham Jones made it seem strange that the beginning of February was too late to try any further amicable methods to solve the dispute.

Extensive management skills, a good sense of humour, intricate knowledge of the Boat Club and no current involvement except for a heart-felt desire to see Oxford successful may well have made Rubin the ultimate mediator. I'm sure his offer was meant with the best intentions, but his outspokenness to the press about 'the structural problems at Oxford. . . echoed by men who rowed in the 1959 crew as well' will have done nothing to endear him to Topolski or McDonald. McDonald never took up his offer to mediate, but his brief involvement did give him the chance to join ranks with the large percentage of the population who had aired their views on the dispute and the topics surrounding it. 'The Boat Race,' he told me, 'should be an under-graduate experience. Graduates make the race a sitting target for dispute because the older guys have already experienced University rowing and have had time to formulate some very accurate opinions on how to get the best results. If things don't match up with their picture, they are ready to question.' After this dispute, many were ready to agree with this opinion.

It is unfortunate that the 1987 dispute was so long and bitter, but it can often take outrage and conflict to generate major changes in a decaying system. This dispute was no exception. Many famous writers and orators have frequently remarked upon this characteristic of the British. 'In England,' philosopher Bertrand Russell once said, 'if you ask for change you will be disregarded at first, persecuted if you persist, but finally canonized if you live long enough!' These American oarsmen fortunately did live long enough to see the changes that they had suggested to make the OUBC a better boat club, come to fruition.

The disregard and persecution of 1987 was rapidly transformed in 1988 and resulted in a major reshuffle of the Boat Club. The reorganisation gave back the Boat Race its clean image and put its management back into the hands of the students. Student control was something that it had been in danger of losing for several years. The race is such a great race and great crowd-puller that it is in constant danger of being exploited by commercial interest. Sponsorship and financial support of the race have become more and more important each year, as the expense of new equipment grows. But those who take part in the race and those who consider themselves responsible for the welfare of the race need to always remember that it is a student race and should remain that way. Too much commercial interest will put the race in danger of losing its greatest attraction, that of being the most perfect of all amateur races.

In an effort to prevent the harmful effects of commercial exploitation, University Boat Clubs in America rely on financial support from their 'Old Boys'. Rubin was clear that the duty of the Old Boy is to provide financial support to allow the clubs to enjoy the finance necessary to run a large and successful club, whilst leaving the club free of the pressures a commercial sponsor may put upon them. Monetary support should be given without any expectation to stay involved in the management of the club. Rubin's philosophy for Old Boys is great, but doesn't seem to be the example followed by our own Universities. We continually fail to drum up the same immense financial support which American sports clubs rely upon.

With ever-increasing demands being made on the Boat Clubs of Oxford and Cambridge as companies fight over the immense publicity which goes with the great race, the University trust fund searches for the money needed to provide new equipment and premises. Today's Oxford Blues agree with Rubin's sentiments, although they must also ask themselves whether they will be prepared to part with the thousands of pounds necessary to keep their University crews afloat when they too are Old Boys.

Questions like these kept the Americans busy whilst their British crewmates fought with themselves and against one or other, trying to form a semblance of a crew for the Boat Race. Few outsiders thought they would win, that is until the very last week before the race. During that week, Topolski and the crew themselves finally began to realise that they could win.

As is so often the case with the Boat Race, it is only the obvious form that is studied and relayed to the interested public. The clear fact was that this crew had not really sorted out their problems. But nobody had noticed that Cambridge were having problems of their own. Oxford had raced and lost to all the good club crews in their first week at Putney: Thames, Imperial and Tideway Scullers had all left them for dead and Hull remembers, 'The more we got beaten, the more we lost hope.' Topolski kicked and cajoled them, moaned at them, scorned them but he never gave up; these were precisely the sort of characteristics that everybody recognised in this Boat Race man and which had caused so many of their earlier problems. For once, though, these characteristics were a bonus. He swapped the crew around the pushed them about, and then finally he took them away from all the pressures of the race by moving upstream to a quieter stretch of the river. Once out of the public eye, with time to stop and think, they suddenly realised there was no time. That it was Cambridge they had to beat, not Topolski and McDonald.

It was a sense of priority that put Oxford back into the picture. They couldn't be forced to realise how important it was for them to win, they needed to work it out for themselves.

Cambridge, meanwhile, were in the sorry position of searching for something they had lost. Their crew had been going fast until two of their best oarsmen, Jim Garman and Jim Pew, were taken ill with chickenpox one month before the race. Richard Spink, the bowman, had injury problems, too; he had had a recurrent problem with his knee which kept him out of the crew on and off throughout the season. In the weeks leading up to the race Cambridge rarely boated with a full crew. This created a particular problem for the coaching team in keeping the oarsmen motivated and clear-headed. It is important in these circumstances that the crew don't focus on the disruptions. This is very hard and was made worse because the press were doing their best to label them as clear favourites for the race.

Mathew Brittin, freshman and junior international, remembered how disconcerting he found the constant changes in the crew, not solely because the crew was constantly in a state of flux, but also because the coaches kept changing the order of the crew. This made it difficult for the oarsmen who rowed right the way through to find anything constant about the crew; every outing seemed as though they were rowing in a scratch combination. When Garman and Pew returned a week before the race, Neil Campbell and Alan Inns put them in at numbers six and seven, two crucial spots in the crew. 'Their rationale,' said Brittin, 'was to use their experience to keep the crew together and keep the stronger boys in the middle, shovelling down the power.' Campbell and Inns also kept experimenting with the strokeman: Brittin started off in the stroke seat, but was then swapped with Peel because they were worried that the stroke position was too much of a responsibility for the young freshman. Peel didn't stay in the stroke seat long, and next they tried Paddy Broughton, who was moved from six to stroke. Despite being a good oarsman, Broughton wasn't renowned for his ability as a strokeman. It takes a particular kind of person to row in the stroke seat, and Broughton, it seems, didn't have that ability. The coaches had their reasons for the constant changes: they were obviously looking for more speed and for 'the best combination'. Brittin and Garman told me that the constant changes were a mistake. Garman and Pew had been very ill but, despite their illness, the coaching team felt they would be better in the crucial positions in the crew. Garman remembers feeling completely inadequate in the race. 'I just wasn't fit enough, you need to be in top condition for a race like the Boat Race, and I wasn't. I'd been ill for too long.' No doubt all of the Cambridge crew could come up with some reason for them losing a race which everybody said they should have won. Brittin relayed the feelings of the whole crew when he said he would always remember it as 'a race which we lost, not one which Oxford won'.

Apart from the problems with the sick crew members there was a noticeable amount of bad planning made by the Cambridge coaching team. Planning is a very important aspect of the Boat Race, not least because of the rapidly changing conditions that the Tideway can produce. On Boat Race day, 1987, it was very rough; Cambridge fitted a pump under the number seven seat to remove excess water from the boat; this was in theory a great idea, but in practice it didn't work because the boat was bow-sectioned. This meant that water which came over the bows and in to the front of the boat was not pumped out, because it was sectioned off from the main portion of the boat where the pump was situated. In the race the bow section rapidly filled up with water whilst the stern section stayed dry, with the result that it left the boat running bows down, encouraging more water to splash in. They also made the mistake of putting five-stay riggers on their boat; in rough conditions these riggers cause water to 'literally pour into the boat', said Mark Lees. Nowadays, both Boat Race crews use the aerofoil riggers designed by Jumbo Edwards to direct the water as much as possible out and not into the boat; under the guidance of Topolski the Oxford crew used them in 1987, giving them another advantage over Cambridge before the crews had even boated. 'The other mistake they made was using carbon-fibre blades instead of the heavier wooden blades,' Lees told me. The type of blades one should use is a source of continual debate between coaches. Carbon-fibre blades are lighter and stiffer than the more traditional wooden blades and are used by almost all international crews nowadays; however, in rough conditions Topolski has always raced his Boat Race crews with wooden blades because their weight stops them being blown around so much, making them easier to control. Lees advocates that he has done some trials on the Tideway which prove easily their superiority when the water is rough (although I doubt that even his experiments will convince those who prefer the carbon-fibre oars). In 1987, Oxford used wooden blades, Cambridge didn't. Lees thinks it gave Oxford at least a two-length advantage. Spracklen, on the other hand, thinks that the most noticeable thing about the Cambridge crew was how low the boat sat in the water. He was watching from Hammersmith when he noticed how low the Cambridge boat sat compared to Oxford's, and realised they must have taken in a lot of water, which added considerably to the weight the crew were having to carry.

Depending upon who you ask why Cambridge were defeated in 1987, the reasons differ; but there is no doubt that a substantial amount of bad planning on their part lost them any edge they may have had, particularly as Topolski had catered for all eventualities. Oxford had three-stay, aerofoil riggers, a big boat and wooden blades: they were all set for rough water. They had a decisive cox, something else Cambridge lacked, and, to cap it all they were the underdogs. Cambridge were hot favourites to win, primarily because of the months of disputing at Oxford. In the race Oxford made use of every advantage possible. Under instruction from Tom Cadoux-Hudson, Lobbenburg headed for the flatter water over near the wall almost as soon as the race began; Cambridge meekly tried to follow. Some say that the move itself gave Oxford a lead, whilst others thought that they gained little in actual distance but a lot in psychological advantage. The Cambridge cox's indecision was bound to have unnerved his crew, whilst Lobbenburg, a determined and decisive character, carried out his actions in the way of a man who means business. Whatever happened, it is the move that the punters will remember most about the race. When the two crews rounded the corner toward the mile post, where they moved back out into the stream, Oxford were fractionally in the lead and had the upper hand. 'There were eight men in that boat all pulling for different reasons, but we all knew that the reasons didn't matter but the way we worked did. It was a sort of amnesty for the day of the race,' said Stewart. 'We did well on the day, and Cambridge did badly.' Cambridge lost to the good crew that everyone had seen through bad luck and bad management. Oxford found the potential which nobody thought they had and, with Topolski's forethought and some excellent coxing, they won the Boat Race. Winning was a triumph, a triumph for Oxford, a triumph for the individuals in the crew, and a triumph for Topolski. That they didn't win with five American internationals on board (and possibly with the fastest Boat Race crew ever) was sad.

The Americans listened to the commentary of the race

on the radio from their respective homes in the US, and Stewart phoned Lyons as soon as he came ashore. The whole crew, with the exception of McDonald, gathered around the telephone as he relayed the story of the race across the world to America. Lyons felt proud that his friends wanted to share their feelings with him: it was a gesture of the long months they had spent training together and of their regret that the Americans had not been a part of the race. Lyons was really glad that they had won; his only sadness was the inevitable summary of the race as a victory for the President. The President's outstretched arms and cries of victory were not only for the joy of beating Cambridge, but were for him a sign of justice, his feelings understandable as he too had suffered an enormous amount of stress over the past few months. Having won, his relief flooded out and sadly he was only too pleased to use the win as a vindication of his management and belief in himself.

It was the fairytale ending that would satisfy the punters. Had the Americans rowed, that too would have been a fairytale ending, but because they didn't the only satisfaction would be if the underdog Oxford crew won. As President he had been given the job of captaining the winning Boat Race crew for Oxford, and he had been successful. It was a shame his success was not celebrated as a sporting victory for the nine men who had raced and won over nine men from Cambridge, as opposed to a win for the President over five Americans at his own University. His attitude left a feeling of distaste with the oarsmen who had helped him to victory: his behaviour was 'unnecessary', said Stewart. 'He would have done well to clear the air and forget the last two months,' Hull stated emphatically. But neither Topolski nor McDonald would do that. Topolski's inherently confrontational nature led him to write his side of the story in his book *True Blue*, and McDonald told *The Guardian* in 1989 that the 'petty hatreds' would 'last all of us for the rest of our lives'. Yet the arguments had never been personal, and the dispute was never meant to be about individuals. That the personalities involved may have widened the gap was secondary to the problems the oarsmen were trying to indicate to their President, when they told him they weren't happy with the way things were being run. That McDonald chose after the race to celebrate the crew's victory as a personal one is sad for the race. The very next term the guardians of the Boat Club, the College Boat Club Captains, condemned that approach and all the egotism that went with it by voting Christopher Penney to be President for the 1988 Boat Race.

16

Voting for the new President of the Oxford University Boat Club is normally a mundane affair; the old President usually nominates one of his squad as his predecessor, another member will second his vote and a show of hands secures the candidate his year of office. There is rarely much competition for the job, the candidate having been chosen by the coaches and oarsmen who rowed in the Blue Boat and been discussed and agreed on before the meeting. Often the candidate is the only Blue to be eligible to race in the following year, or the only man who wants the job. In McDonald's year, Clark and he were both eligible but only McDonald wanted the job.

Voting is by a show of hands after the candidate has briefly outlined to the voters his ideas and plans for the coming year; there is rarely any dispute. Predictably, however, after the 1987 race there were two candidates nominated for the position of President: the first, nominated by McDonald, was Tom Cadoux-Hudson; the second, nominated by Hull, was Chris Penney. Penney was the only one of the Americans who would be returning to Oxford for the following academic year.

Prior to the meeting there was a private war being waged by two campaigners. While on one of the infamous Boat Club trips where the OUBC is invited to send a crew, expenses paid, to a regatta in some far-off sunny place to race, Pelham told the crew that McDonald had asked Cadoux-Hudson to be President. He had not asked the opinion of the rest of the crew, but had 'steam-rollered everything through in typical McDonald fashion', claimed Hull. Cadoux-Hudson, however, wanted to know if the guys were happy with him as President, which is the reason why Pelham was asking around.

'It wasn't that we didn't want Cadoux-Hudson as President, but that we felt that decisions were being made behind our backs yet again. Normally it is a group decision to decide who should be nominated as President,' explained Ward. Back in Britain at the start of Trinity Term, the Americans saw their chance to revive in the Boat Race the ideals which had enticed them to the race in the first place. Chris Penney was returning next year, and in him it was easy to recognise the perfect President. He is a top class oarsman who started his rowing career within the University system. He was well-known and liked by the College Captains and many college oarsmen because much of his spare time was spent on the river, rowing or coaching for his college. He had spoken at the Union and was a respected academic and leader, so it was put to him that he should stand as President. Penney wasn't sure at first. He, like Cadoux-Hudson, had had enough of fighting and wanted to be sure that people were keen on the idea of his standing.

In their insistance for legitimate support, both Cadoux-Hudson and Penney were steering the beginnings of next year's Boat Race toward being the student-controlled race it was supposed to be. Neither Penney nor Cadoux-Hudson wanted to canvas for support, but their 'guardians' most certainly did: particularly Fish and Lyons, who are in their element when on a mission to see their visions fulfilled. They looked first of all to the support of Stewart, Ward and Hull. Having supported them in their disagreements over Ward's selection, they hoped that they could count on their support. Stewart was unsure. 'I was emotionally drained, and electing Penney was a controversial idea. I just didn't want to elect him and then be involved in the responsibility of clearing up after the last mess.' Stewart said he was going to vote for Cadoux-Hudson, and took a lot of flack for saying so.

'We, all of the oarsmen I mean, finally had the chance to do something constructive, to change the things that had been wrong last year, but the zest had gone and we weren't getting the support we wanted,' said Fish. It was frustrating and hard for them to understand how much support they had given each other in the dispute when there was almost no hope of defeating Topolski or McDonald, but now that they had a real chance they reached out for it with the energy they became known for. Despite initial resistance, the preparation and effort that Penney and Fish and Lyons put in paid off. By the time of the meeting they had sounded out coaches, agreed that Spracklen would be Chief Coach for the Blue Boat, prepared a list of the changes they thought needed to be made to the Constitution and thought out how college rowing could be improved and generally researched and co-ordinated. A skeleton plan of action was created.

At the meeting, when McDonald presented Cadoux-Hudson as a *fait accompli* to the Captains, there was a lot to be said, not only by those directly involved in the dispute, but by members of the squad who had reserved their judgements until then. Hull stood and nominated Penney; Pete Gish volunteered his support for Penney, 'in view of McDonald's complete mismanagement last year,' he said. Penney finally brought himself to the fore with a strident speech outlining his ideas and idealism for the coming year. But it was Tony Ward who finally swayed the Captains: he spoke directly and honestly, because he believed Penney was the best man for the job, and he came across as the sort of person who only does things because he believes them to be right. A secret ballot was used for the first time, so that the Captains and old Blues in residence could feel free to vote for whoever they chose, and Penney was voted in by 27 votes to 19. Stewart did in the end vote for Penney, mostly because he had Penney's word that Spracklen was going to coach, but his sympathies lay with Tom, who he said would have made a good President. Undoubtedly both men were qualified for the job, but the Boat Club was in need of a shakeup, and the voters obviously felt that Penney was more likely to do that. 'Tom was quite a closet radical in his own right,' said Hull, 'but Penney had more time, more idealism and an inherently amiable nature which gave him the edge for the job.'

'Tom would have been good, but Penney was great,' said Ward. And so it was: Penney was the 1988 President of the

Oxford University Boat Club.

The news made the sports pages of all the papers in America and Britain, particularly since Topolski and McDonald were outspoken about their outrage at the result. 'To elect someone not involved in the race is perverse,' Topolski told the *Herald Tribune*. Not perverse, but new perhaps, although to say that Penney had not been involved in the race was perhaps more perverse than his election as President!

A new year and new ideas, and there was a lot of work to be done. Suddenly the Boat Club belonged to the students again. It was a 'tremendous feeling for us all', said Lyons and everybody wanted to help. Summer Eights and the college bumping races are the new President's first official duty. Then there is the Henley Royal Regatta, which the Boat Club tries to support by producing crews from the previous year's Boat Race crews, and any new members of the squad who are considering trying out for the Boat Race next year. Of course, next year must be carefully thought out: the coaches, the training venues, the oarsmen, and finally any major changes which the President might wish to make. This would include changes to the Boat Club Constitution and an effort to integrate college oarsmen into a development squad to strengthen the standard of rowers trying for the Boat Race crews, also to strengthen the standard of rowing at college level by insisting that trial oarsmen take part in the college bumps races in Hilary Term. Penney had so many ideas, and a year to get them started. Much to Penney's delight, Fish had decided at his own expense to return to Oxford for another year to help Penney sort out the organisational problems which may crop up in such a busy year, and also to help coach. He was to be invaluable in coming up with the ideas and help which the Boat Club definitely needed. Fish made it his job to drum up as much support for the new system as he could. He made use of the flash image the Boat Race has to get people who had no interest in actually rowing to come and help with the organisation. 'The Boat Race is such a prestigious event that I had no trouble using to get people involved in setting up the race, and Topolski would have had even less trouble; it's just that he hadn't thought of using non-rowers to help before. He is a smooth and charismatic guy, and had he thought of it he would have had no trouble drumming up the support I found.'

Steven Royle in his new job, employed as Administrator to the Boat Club, joined in and instantly set about clearing up the turmoil of the past few years. 'The administration was in a mess: nobody knew what equipment the club owned, where it was being kept, or even what the club's quite large sums of money were being spent on. My first priority was to get that side of things under control so that the future Presidents and their oarsmen would know exactly what they had available to them to run their Boat Club. Topolski had given the Boat Club an image which the Boat Club had thrived on and flourished under for twelve years, but he had lost touch of what was going on at the oarsman's level. The day-to-day management had drifted, and the race had lost its interest for the oarsmen themselves. It was Topolski's race during his years as chief coach, not the students' race, and I saw one of my important duties being to give the race back to them.'

To get things moving, Penney had two major changes to work on; firstly, he wanted to make it clear that rowing at a college level was maintained. He thought that OUBC should encourage the development of college rowing by not taking all the good oarsmen away from their college boat clubs, but by trying to encourage the better rowers to give some input back to their college clubs. Complementary to this, he wanted to encourage the influx of more unknown potential from the colleges to filter in to the Boat Race squads. It had been a major complaint of the OUBC that the system took from the colleges but did nothing to support them. The second aspect he needed to work on was changing Boat Race training and coaching. This was relatively easy to plan, once the help of Spracklen had been assured.

When Penney initially contacted Mike he refused to be involved in the position of Chief Coach because he already had a lot on his plate preparing Britain's Olympic Team. However, he was keen to support Penney; he didn't think that the Americans were the black sheep that people made them out to be. 'I don't think I know a more gentlemanly gentleman than Chris,' Mike told me. When Penney persisted, Spracklen eventually agreed, although he laid down several provisos. He said he could only coach every afternoon, but not at weekends, he couldn't coach Isis, and he also stipulated that Royle should be supported as Administrator and Topolski should be asked to coach. Firstly because, he said, 'he is Oxford and secondly because it would repair a lot of damage, and finally, but not least, because he's a good coach'. Penney objected because he said he didn't feel that he could trust Topolski, but Spracklen insisted and Topolski was duly asked to coach. Both Penney and Spracklen rang Topolski, but to no avail; he wasn't available to coach Oxford for the 1988 Boat Race. Satisfied that he had tried to get Topolski back to Oxford, and happy that he made his conditions of coaching quite clear, Spracklen became Chief Coach.

Spracklen ran the Oxford squad the same way as he ran his national team: the technique and training employed were entirely up to him to specify, but it was Penney's job to make sure everybody knew what was going on. A meeting between Fish, Penney, Spracklen and Royle, almost as soon as the elections were over, outlined the major complaints that the oarsmen wanted to avoid. They wanted more continuity in the coaching. That was easy to solve: with Spracklen coaching in the afternoons and Fish also coaching daily, there was immediate consistency. They wanted to know which technique was to be followed. As a master of technique, Spracklen had already produced a booklet on technique, and this was handed out to all the oarsmen. They wanted to organise their training so that it didn't directly interfere with a whole day. A programme was worked out whereby the crews trained in the gym in the early morning rather than directly after rowing in the evenings. Rowing, too, was organised so that endless time was not wasted travelling around. Royle's new full-time post made these organisational changes more logistically possible, and Spracklen's workouts meant time on the water was efficient, hard training, ninety-five per cent of it coached.

In a short time, Penney, Fish, Royle and Spracklen had shaken up the Boat Club and its old regimes. The actual training programmes were written by Royle and Spracklen in combination. Spracklen wrote a skeleton and requested a certain type of work, and then Royle filled in the content. The gym tests and timed runs were cut, as were maximum weight circuits. For the first term they rowed between 1pm and 4pm six days a week, and did two weight circuits in the early mornings; these were medium weights with lots of repetitions, aimed at fitness. Much of the rowing was in Pairs. The combinations of the Pairs changed frequently so that by Christmas the individuals all knew who were the best men; everyone had rowed together in all sorts of Pair combinations. The training was very competitive, and so, by the time it came to select the crews, the actual naming of the crew was more of a formality. It is easy to see who comes out best when Pair combinations are constantly changed in training. This is the method Spracklen likes to use to select his crews for the World Championships.

During the second term, the weights sessions were cut and the crew trained once a day, still on six days per week. The crews were coached daily and the progress monitored continually by those coaches involved. When the crew was finally selected only one person asked to be Seat Raced, and that was Justin Cheetle. He had had glandular fever and wanted a chance to demonstrate his fitness. Spracklen says he wouldn't have bothered, feeling that he wasn't good enough to merit a place anyway, but Penney and Fish made a point of letting him be raced. The race was as expected, Cheetle lost, but at least everyone was happy that the selection was fair.

Spracklen wasn't in charge of Isis, and Penney remembered that that was the major change that they got wrong by using Spracklen's selection methods. There was a lot of talent available that year, as there had been the year before, and the racing in Pairs meant that the good oarsmen who realised they weren't going to make the Blue Boat realised this a bit earlier than they would have done using Topolski's methods. Some of those people then gave up instead of rowing in Isis. By Christmas no-one had been selected, but it was obvious who was going to make it and who wasn't; if it had been less obvious until half-way through the next term, those few probably would have continued training and would have been available to row in Isis, feeling that it was worth carrying on since the race was only a few weeks away. 'It was better for their academic careers that they drop out of the squad if they weren't going to make the Blue Boat, but it wasn't quite what we had in mind for developing a strong Isis squad,' said Fish.

The Boat Race crew for 1988 was duly formed, and did an impressive job of beating Cambridge without coaching from any particular Boat Race 'specialists'. As much as was possible, the crews were coached and trained like any other crew for any other important race. The basis of this training regime is still being used in Oxford today. Spracklen was chief coach just for 1988, but in 1989 and 1990 he came back to coach for a couple of weeks in the winter, and to coach the last two weeks before the race. The same type of work programme is still being used: outings are in the afternoons for most of the year, the gym happens before lectures in the mornings, and the crews have one day off a week. The coaching team changes slightly from year to year, but continuity remains the major theme. The new system has not changed everything, but seeks to make best use of the good parts of the old system whilst ensuring that the Boat Club stays abreast of new developments in rowing and training methods, most of all accommodating the changing student academic lifestyle. Within this structure there is still an important role for the real Boat Race enthusiasts like the John Pilgrim-Morrises of the world, whose time spent coaching and helping the Boat Race crews over the years makes their enthusiasm and dedication to the sport undeniably important.

There is perhaps one real similarity in the coaching of today's Boat Race crews with those of the past. Since Topolski left and the dispute kick-started a change in the organisation and image of the race, Royle has tried to continue that development by getting Britain's top coaches involved in the main body of the crew development. In 1988 and 1989 they had Spracklen, in 1990 they invested in Patrick Sweeney, who worked with Spracklen as cox and coach producing the national teams for the 1984 and 1988 Olympics and the intervening World Championships. The only difference between this and the old Boat Race coaches is that in the past the Oxford coaches were Oxford first.

When Fish first arrived at Oxford and walked down the towpath to the boathouses, he remembers the vision that the abundance of oarsmen and boats and coaches gave him: 'I knew that there must be so much talent here,' but he couldn't see it. So many people row and train hard at their rowing at Oxford, he was convinced that Oxford should easily be able to produce any number of crews to beat any Junior Varsity crew the Americans might produce. But he's seen Oxford Boat Race crews get beaten by some of the worst US college crews. Oxford college crews would be annihilated by many US Junior Varsity crews. 'The talent wasn't being directed, and some potential Boat Race material', he felt, was being wasted. Trying to capture some of that talent was another goal that Penney tried to fulfil. His plan was to set up a development squad from college oarsmen who wanted to trial and who would go through a similar process of selection for the development squad as they would for the Boat Race. They started the development squad by holding an open day, to which any oarsman was entitled to come. They had a turnout of 130 rowers. After a series of coaching sessions and much thought, a group of oarsmen who they thought would make potentially good oarsmen were selected; they made it quite clear that they weren't trying to select the best eight oarsmen, but oarsmen who potentially could be good. It was a new concept and was successful in that they found a few rowers who did go on to row in the Boat Race and trial for the British National team. 'But the squad was unsuccessful in its first year,' said Fish, because they failed to take keenness into account. The squad needed something more concrete than learning to row to motivate them. 'The basis of the idea was there, and the colleges were keen for it to work because we worked into the plan an obligation for the development squad men to row for their colleges in "Torpids", which meant that whilst they were getting good coaching from the University coaches, they were feeding that back into the college by continuing to row with them.' In the second year the idea was developed more, with keenness taken into account. The squad produced an Eight and a Coxed Four which stayed together right through the year until Henley Royal Regatta. In terms of the Boat Race, the benefits of the scheme have not yet been fully appreciated because there is still a big influx into Oxford of top-class oarsmen and ex-junior Internationals who obviously are keen to row in the Boat Race. But there will soon be a year when there will be little proven talent, and those who are responsible for the birth and maintenance of the scheme are confident that the development squad will then come to fruition. College rowing is the backbone of University rowing, and in the past some coaches have tended to forget that. Penney realised the importance and encouraged it, as did many other Boat Race oarsmen.

Apart from the rowing, there were other changes which Penney wanted to make to the Boat Club. These were changes to the Constitution aimed at up-dating the antiquated document which had been their downfall the previous year. Hull, who was Penney's Vice-President, was mainly responsible for producing the new document. In it, the Oxford University Boat Club was given an umbrella rowing club which is called the Oxford University Rowing Club. This umbrella covers the four University boat clubs, the men's and women's heavyweight boat clubs and the men's and women's lightweight boat clubs. Each has a University crew which is selected and races against Cambridge in a Boat Race. The men's and women's lightweight and women's heavyweight Boat Races are held annually at Henley on Thames. The men's heavyweight Boat Race is the race we all know as the Oxford and Cambridge Boat Race. The President of the OURC is the President of the Oxford University Boat Club, and Steve Royle is employed as Administrator for the umbrella club, although his priority is to the men's Boat Race crews. Royle's appointment is supported by the aims of the OUBC, which are to run the college rowing and to 'encourage the development of men's and women's heavyweight and lightweight rowing at Oxford'. It has a committee of its own which runs the organisation of the college bumps races, although the President retains some responsibility by having overall charge. The changes have given more people a chance to be involved in the organisation of the rowing, thus spreading the load. The colleges saw some immediate advantages in the new system, as did the OUBC; the lightweight and women's heavyweight boat clubs are now beginning to see the justification for having a joint rowing club, as the OURC now ensures that they have more money and more coching support to run their teams. Eventually, Royle hopes to see all four clubs running with a system such as the OUBC now has, and with sufficient funding and direction to have a real impact on the respective clubs. The OURC has a mission to give all rowers an equal standing in the University, instead of leaving the lightweight and women's heavyweight crews as poor cousins. The other lauded addition to the new Constitution was a clause which allowed the President to be removed from power should an extraordinary meeting be called by the Boat Club captains. A written request containing the signatures of six Captains of Boats would still be required to call such a meeting, but the President must then convene the meeting within forty-eight hours of the request. The changes to the Constitution were small, but made important decisions more democratic, and more importantly made it possible to dispense of anyone holding the office of President should this become necessary.

So what did the Boat Race oarsmen think, was it better or was it chaos? Stewart's impressions are important because he learnt to row at Oxford, spent three years trying to make the Boat Race then, once he made it, he rowed in Isis and the Blue Boat under Topolski, and then in 1988 in the Blue Boat under Spracklen; he'd seen it all. 'The land training was efficient, the logistics worked well, everyone knew what was happening when, and Penney was like a rock in the middle of the boat, as a President should be.' What more could he say? 'Oh,' he added, 'and Fish was great; he was there every day finding out what was going wrong and what was right!' And they won the Boat Race.

Royle still hopes that one day Topolski will be persuaded to return to coach the Boat Race crews for Oxford, not in the same way he took over before, but 'so that we can use his own special magic for the last few weeks before the race'. Royle is full of hope for Topolski to return because he feels that in the stability of the new system, he would be in his element. 'Having him on the coaching team is as much a psychological weapon against the opposition, and he is useful to make a big difference to the pure speed of the crew.' But for the moment, Topolski has not returned, and Oxford is content with Spracklen's equally captivating magic. But to a certain extent, the job of the coach is to melt into the background, for it is the magic of the many students who take part in this race each year that make the race special. Each one of them different in person and in ability, but each of them contributing their bit toward keeping the race in the tradition of its origin, beginning with the sort of people who row for fun or because they like it, then enjoy winning and want to race in the Boat Race of Oxford versus Cambridge, which is a race about winning and losing: but perhaps even more about the people who win it.

ACKNOWLEDGEMENTS

I would like to thank Larry Tracy for making this book possible; my family and friends, without whose contributions and encouragement this book would never have been written; the eight men whose story has now been told: Christopher Clark, Jon Fish, Christopher Huntington, Richard Hull, Dan Lyons, Christopher Penney, Gavin Stewart and Tony Ward; Dr Michael Barry for allowing me access to the Oxford University Boat Club Constitution; Peter Spurrier for the excellent photographs; and, for their time and enthusiasm, Richard Ayling, Simon Berrisford, Mathew Brittin, Tom Cadoux-Hudson, Christopher Dodd, Richard Fishlock, Paul Gleeson, Jim Garman, Steven Kiesling, Mark Lees, Stephen Peel, Hugh Pelham, John Pilgrim-Morris, Steven Redgrave, Steven Royle, Reed Rubin, Freddie Smallbone, Mike Spracklen and James Svenson-Taylor.